The Coolest People in the Performing Arts: 250 Anecdotes and Stories

David Bruce

Published by David Bruce, 2024.

While every precaution has been taken in the preparation of this book, the publisher assumes no responsibility for errors or omissions, or for damages resulting from the use of the information contained herein.

THE COOLEST PEOPLE IN THE PERFORMING ARTS: 250 ANECDOTES AND STORIES

First edition. November 18, 2024.

Copyright © 2024 David Bruce.

ISBN: 979-8230373421

Written by David Bruce.

Table of Contents

Chapter 1: From Anger to Costumes 1
Chapter 2: From Critics to Food 16
Chapter 3: From Friends to Mishaps 31
Chapter 5: From Publicity to Work 60
Appendix A: Bibliography 75
Appendix B: About the Author 83
Appendix C: Some Books by David Bruce 84

Dedication

Dedicated to Amateur and Professional Creative People
Rise above.

Theater director Tyrone Guthrie advised his actors and crew to do this. The advice means to rise above whatever forces are working against you. All of us have personal problems. No one's life is perfect. Sometimes, life seems to conspire against us. Rise above all that, and produce the best work you can.

Astonish me.

Dance impresario Sergei Diaghilev advised his choreographers to do this. The advice means what it says. Do such good work that the person who commissioned the work — and of course the audience — is astonished. (Tyrone Guthrie also used this phrase.)

Do it now.

As a young man, choreographer George Balanchine nearly died and so he believed in living his life day by day and not holding anything back. He would tell his dancers, "Why are you stingy with yourselves? Why are you holding back? What are you saving for — for another time? There are no other times. There is only now. Right now." Throughout his career, including before he became world renowned, he worked with what he had, not complaining about wanting a bigger budget or better dancers. One of the pieces of advice Mr. Balanchine gave over and over was this: "Do it now."

Go out and get one.

Ruth St. Denis once taught Martha Graham an important lesson when Ms. Graham was just starting to dance. Ms. St. Denis told Ms. Graham, "Show me your dance." Ms. Graham replied, "I don't have one," and Ms. St. Denis advised, "Well, dear, go out and *get* one." (Everyone needs an art to practice. Your art need not be dance. Perhaps your art can be writing autobiographical essays. Of course, you may practice more than one art.)

Assign yourself.

The parents of Marian Wright Edelman were serious about education. Each school night, she and her siblings were expected to sit down and do their homework. Whenever one of the children said that the teacher had not assigned any homework, her father used to say, "Well, assign yourself." Ms. Edelman once made out a list of "Twenty-Five Lessons for Life," based on the values she had learned from her parents. Lesson 3 was, "Assign yourself. Don't wait around to be told what to do." In 1973, she founded the Children's Defense Fund, which attempts to get federal legislation passed to help children.

Challenge yourself.

Joss Whelon created the TV series *Buffy the Vampire Slayer*, which is noted for its clever dialogue. Day after day, people told Joss that they watched the series because of its dialogue, so he decided to challenge himself by writing an episode in which the characters could not talk. The episode, titled "Hush," is excellent and was nominated for an Emmy.

Practice an art.

The father of choreographer Bella Lewitzky taught her the importance of having an art to practice. He worked at an ordinary job, but when he came home, he painted. Ms. Lewitzky says, "He taught me that it didn't make a d*mn bit of difference what you did for a living, as long as you had something that rewarded your life." He also didn't feel that it was necessary to have an audience for his art because the act of creation was rewarding in itself. Bella and her sister used to steal their father's paintings — because if they didn't, he would paint another work of art on top of the one he had already created.

Do it yourself.

Early in their career, the Ramones played in London on July 4, 1976. Some cool kids who called themselves The Clash hung around during a sound check before the concert and talked to the members of the band, mentioning that they played music but weren't good enough to play in public. Johnny Ramone told them, "Are you kidding? I hope you're coming tonight. We're lousy. We can't play. If you wait until you can play, you'll be too old to get up there. We stink, really. But it's great." (This is a great example of punk rock's do-it-yourself attitude. You don't need a lot of fancy equipment to play music. Just teach yourself a few chords, get up on stage, and rock. Similarly, if you want to write, you don't need a lot of fancy equipment. If you have a computer, great, but all you really need is some paper and a pencil or pen.)

Be there.

After retiring from her career in dance, Balanchine dancer Barbara Milberg became a very good student — and eventually a Ph.D. (and professor). In dance, she had learned that when the curtain went up, she had better be there, and so she never handed in a paper late.

Get it right.

A man — who didn't dance — visited the dance class of Margaret Craske. At the end of her class, he said goodbye and jokingly executed a *port de bras*. Quickly, Ms. Craske reached out and corrected the position of the visitor's hand. As you would expect, in her dance classes, she tells her students over and over, "Get it right!"

Cover Photograph for The Coolest People in the Performing Arts: Public Domain

George Balanchine

https://en.wikipedia.org/wiki/George_Balanchine#/media/File:Portrait_of_Ringling_Circus_choreographer_George_Balanchine.jpg

Educate Yourself

Read Like A Wolf Eats

Be Excellent to Each Other

Books Then, Books Now, Books Forever

Chapter 1: From Anger to Costumes

Anger
• Early in her career, lieder singer Lotte Lehmann often grew angry at Dr. Hans Loewenfeld, director of the Hamburg Municipal Theater, and wrote angry letters to him. Dr. Loewenfeld knew that Ms. Lehmann's anger would quickly blow over and so the letters were not meant to be taken personally; still, he had a whole collection of angry letters from her. When Ms. Lehmann left the Hamburg Municipal Theater to join the Vienna Court Opera, he told her that he had kept the letters so that he could read them when he was in a "bad temper." Her final teasing comment to him before she left was, "So now I know that you'll often think of me."[1]

• Choreographer George Balanchine seldom got angry, but one time he did get angry was immediately before a performance when he saw a stagehand drop cigar ashes on a freshly mopped floor. He yelled at the stagehand, "Don't you know where you are? You're not in the street! This is not a gutter! This is the theater—a place where people *dance*!"[2]

Animals
• Mid-1950s Metropolitan Opera basso Gerhard Pechner enjoyed taking care of animals. If he found a hurt animal, he did his best to care for it. One day, on his way to the Met for a rehearsal of *Parsifal*, he found a pigeon with a hurt wing in the snow. Putting it in his breast pocket, he continued to the Met. During rehearsal, he always kept at least one hand on the pigeon to keep it from being frightened. However, at this rehearsal, he was expected to act, and the conductor, Fritz Stiedry, kept asking him to take both hands out of his pocket. Finally, Mr. Stiedry asked, "Can't you raise both hands at once?" Then Mr. Pechner was forced to reveal the hurt pigeon to the other artists. He says, "You should have heard the shouts from that *Parsifal* cast."[3]

- Suzanne Farrell danced the role of Titania in *A Midsummer Night's Dream*, in which she fell in love with the ass-headed Bottom. Someone suggested that she treat Bottom as if he were a pussy cat, and Suzanne immediately went out and got a cat, which she named Bottom. At first, her mother did not want the cat around, but eventually she grew to love cats and got one of her own, which she named Top. Sometimes, when Suzanne and her cat Bottom were together, her mother used to joke, "Let me kiss my baby goodbye," and then ignore Suzanne and instead kiss the cat.[4]
- Joan Hammond was a great lover of dogs. Some mischievous boys once threw a stick into the Thames River and her beloved French poodle "Pippo" jumped in. Unfortunately, the river current was swift and Pippo soon had trouble staying afloat, so Ms. Hammond jumped in—fully clothed—and rescued him.[5]

Audiences
- In 2009, Frederic Franklin at age 94 was still on stage with American Ballet Theatre. In his long career, he danced with many notables, including a half-naked Josephine Baker. For a while, he performed in an ensemble with Alicia Markova and Anton Dolin in provincial music halls. On one occasion, when he came onstage wearing tights, the audience shouted, "He's wearing his granny's underwear." He had been a principal dancer with the Ballet Russe de Monte Carlo, and on one occasion their dance concert was received by the audience with total silence. Afterwards, Mr. Franklin said to a member of the audience, "I don't think you enjoyed the performance—there was no applause." She replied, "Oh we did, but it was all so nice we didn't want to disturb the atmosphere." Seraphine Astafieva was the teacher of the great Anton Dolin. As a youth, he saw her dance in the Swinburne Ballet, then he immediately told his mother, "I will and must learn to dance in her school."[6]
- Olga Spessivtzeva once made an unkind remark about Vera Trefilova. Ms. Trefilova had balanced for a very long time on one *pointe*

in arabesque while partnered by Pierre Vladimirov in *The Sleeping Beauty* in London at the Alhambra Theatre during the 1921-1922 season of Sergei Diaghilev's ballet company. Ms. Spessivtzeva said that it was a "trick," adding, "She just balances against Vladimirov's thigh." Ms. Trefilova heard about the remark, so at her next performance of *The Sleeping Beauty*, she repeated the "trick"—but this time Mr. Vladimirov stood far away from her, making it impossible for her to balance against his knee. In his biography *Olga Spessivtzeva*, Anton Dolin wrote, "The audience went wild with amazement, and an audible gasp went through the theatre, ending in a frenzy of applause. I was there, on stage, and saw it myself."[7]

****

• Tap dancer Bunny Briggs once was feeling really good during his act. He noticed a man sitting by a woman, and he told the man, "Why don't you put your arm around the lady? Enjoy yourself. You're sittin' there with your hands folded." Mr. Briggs started dancing to "I'll Be Loving You, Always," then he said, "Dim the lights." At this point, all the men in the audience put their arms around the women they were with. Seeing this, Mr. Briggs said, "This is the first and last time I'll ask for this. I don't want no applause. Just stay like that." He then danced a little more, and went off to complete silence, because all the men and women in the audience were hugging and kissing. This, says Mr. Briggs, was the greatest compliment he ever received as a dancer.[8]

• Subscribers to the Metropolitan Opera really do support the Met. On one occasion, an opera had many problems with many cancellations and many substitutions, and the lead soprano who ended up singing on a certain night—at the last minute—gave a very bad performance. Critic Patrick J. Smith was sure that the subscribers would protest, but instead he discovered that they understood the problems that that particular opera faced and so they rallied around the Met and did not complain.[9]

- Not every dance affects the audience the way the dancer/choreographer wants it to. Paul Sanasardo choreographed three solos about death titled collectively *Three Dances of Death* (1956). The third solo was "The Sentimentalist," and when he danced it, he was surprised by the audience's reaction: They laughed. When he finished the solo, the great choreographer Paul Taylor, who was also dancing on the program, told him, "That's a really funny dance." Not surprisingly, that was the last time Mr. Sanasardo danced the solo.[10]
- Marie Taglioni was a well-loved ballet dancer. In Russia, her carriage was stopped by robbers who recognized her and told her that she could keep her jewels and money if she danced for them. So on rugs spread over the muddy ground, Ms. Taglioni danced for them. Later, she said, "I never had such an appreciative audience either before or afterwards." In Paris, after she had danced, the curtain could not be brought down because her adoring fans had thrown such a thick layer of flowers on the stage.[11]
- Ballet dancer Rudolf Nureyev's temper was world famous. In Chicago, he was suffering from a torn calf muscle, and it took him a long time to warm it for a performance. The audience grew restless and started clapping for the show to start, so Mr. Nureyev stepped in front of the curtain and shouted, "Everyone, shut up!" They did, and they were pleased that night to witness both one of Mr. Nureyev's performances and one of his legendary bursts of temper.[12]
- Anna Pavlova danced "The Dying Swan" thousands of times, but occasionally she was not pleased with the audience's always-thunderous applause. After one performance that did not reach her own high standard, she was very angry about the applause and complained, "How dare they applaud like that. I know I danced badly. It is no compliment to an artist. I shall lose all my standards, if people aren't more discriminating."[13]
- George Balanchine choreographed *Liebeslieder Walzer* in such a way that some members of the audience regarded it as a series of

"love-song waltzes," and some members of early audiences would leave the theater between acts. Lincoln Kirstein once watched the audience between acts, and he moaned to Mr. Balanchine, "Look how many people are leaving." Unperturbed, Mr. Balanchine replied, "Ah, but look how many are staying!"[14]

• In 1910, at an opera house in Vercelli, Piedmont, Italy, Tito Schipa sang the part of Alfredo in his first *La Traviata*. At the time, he had a very slight build, but the diva playing Violetta was very large. As Violetta crushed Alfredo to her bosom, a man in the audience shouted, "Don't crush the poor boy—we want to hear him sing!"[15]

• When Rudolph Nureyev and Margot Fonteyn danced *Giselle* with the Royal Ballet in Los Angeles, a man in the audience watched Mr. Nureyev dance and then asked his wife who he was. She said, "That is the man who jumped over the Berlin Wall." He replied, "No wonder he jumped over the wall, if he can jump like that!"[16]

Automobiles

• Four soloists—Rudolph Nureyev, Rosella Hightower, Erik Bruhn, and Sonia Arova—formed their own dance company and went on tour. Along the coast from Marseilles to Cannes, the car the company was traveling in broke down, leaving them stuck along the roadside until 4 a.m. Fortunately, the only member of the company with any mechanical ability was able to fix the car—Rosella Hightower.[17]

• Performing artists often travel by car. During his career, Merce Cunningham choreographed many dances for quartets and quintets. Asked why, Mr. Cunningham replied that only four or five people can fit in a station wagon that is already loaded with sets and costumes.[18]

Children

• One of dancer Nick Florez' biggest boosters was Sandra, his big sister. At age six, he loved to dance, and so Sandra, who was 14 and had no driver's license, drove him to town from their chicken farm in Texas (the distance was too great to walk) and signed him up for dance lessons. Later, when Nick was 13, Sandra learned that the Chuck E. Cheese restaurants in Dallas were looking for children to dance in videos that the restaurants would show. She let Nick know about the opportunity, and he became one of the children to pass the audition. Nick said, "We filmed about eight videos. By the last ones, I was helping choreograph them. I'd make up some parts on my own and show them to the producers. They loved it." Nick has danced on tour and in music videos for such stars as Janet Jackson, Jordan Knight, Selena, Smashmouth, Will Smith, Britney Spears, and others.[19]

• Several children studied and danced with Paul Sanasardo and Donya Feuer at the Studio for Dance in New York City, and as adults many of them still studied and danced with them. Judith Blackstone remembers spending Saturday afternoons as a child with Mr. Sanasardo and Bill Weaver, an actor and stage manager. Mr. Sanasardo had many art books, and Mr. Weaver would hold her in his lap and they would look at artworks by Paul Gauguin together. Another child dancer, Lynn Barr, remembers that Mr. Sanasardo and Ms. Feuer had a wonderful life filled with wonderful dance, art, and music, and she was disappointed to grow up and realize that not every adult lived that way. As an adult, she said, "They were the only two people who never compromised."[20]

• Rudolf Nureyev lived in Ufa, a small town but one that had an opera house. When he was seven years old, his mother bought one ticket to a ballet at the opera house and snuck in the entire family—the Nureyevs had little money. Young Rudolf saw the ballet *The Song of the Cranes* and immediately decided to devote his life to dance. In a review of Julie Kavanagh's book *Nureyev: The Life*, Joan Acocella wrote in *The New Yorker*, "In dance biographies, one hears suspiciously often of these thunderclaps, but I think they should be credited if they are soon followed by intense study." In young Rudolf's case, his thunderclap was in fact soon followed by intense study.[21]

• Beth Joiner, a children's dance teacher in Georgia, once had a problem with a young student who talked continually about her boyfriend. Finally, Miss Beth explained that the constant talk about the boyfriend was getting silly and interfering with the dance class. Aghast, the student replied, "Miss Beth, in the third grade, boyfriends may be silly, but in the fourth grade, they are serious business." Ms. Joiner has learned that occasionally her youngest students will go to the bathroom, then return to class five minutes later, wearing their leotards around their ankles.[22]

• Enrico Caruso's little son, Mimmi, wanted to show his famous father to his friends. A number of Mimmi's friends came to visit him, and he asked his father to come into the room where they had gathered. There Mr. Caruso saw that they were listening to a record by Henry Lauder, a Scottish entertainer who sang popular songs. Mr. Caruso asked Mimmi, "You like Harry Lauder records?" Mimmi replied, "Oh, yes. We like them much better than Caruso records." His little playmates agreed with Mimmi.[23]

• At a dress rehearsal of *The Barber of Seville* in La Scala, Plácido Domingo and his family sat together in a box to watch. Placi, his son, began applauding and calling "Bravo" too loudly, and so an usher said that he had to leave. Mr. Domingo's father commented, "Unfortunately, at La Scala, Placi cannot say, 'They've thrown me out of better theatres than this one.'"[24]

• Children have priorities, too. When they were young, a brother and a sister, dancer Olympia Dowd and guitarist Dylan Dowd, were given a choice by their parents. They could have either a trampoline or a TV. Olympia and Dylan opted for the trampoline.[25]

Choreographers

• Choreographer George Balanchine disliked the star system in which one or a few dancers were the stars of a dance troupe; therefore, he disliked it when Serge Lifar became the star dancer of Serge Diaghilev's dance troupe. When Mr. Balanchine choreographed *Prodigal Son*, he told Mr. Lifar that at one point he wanted him to fall flat on his back. Mr. Lifar did not want to do that because, as he pointed out, it would hurt his back. However, Mr. Balanchine responded that it would not hurt at all and that he would demonstrate how Mr. Lifar should fall. Mr. Balanchine then fell on his back and got up, smiling. Later, Mr. Balanchine admitted that the fall had "hurt like hell! But I had to do only once, and Lifar, he must do *every night*!"[26]

• When Léonide Massine was a young dancer with Serge Diaghilev Ballets-Russes, he and Mr. Diaghilev went to the Uffizi, where they looked at Fra Filippo Lippi's *Madonna and Child*. Mr. Diaghilev asked, "Do you think you could compose a ballet?" Mr. Massine had never choreographed before, so he answered, "No. I'm sure I never could." Then Mr. Massine looked at Simone Martini's *Annunciation*, and he said, "Yes. I think I can create a ballet. Not only one, but a hundred, I promise you."[27]

• When Peter Martins choreographed Stravinski's *Eight Easy Pieces* for two pianos, he wanted to use three New York City Ballet ballerinas, but George Balanchine vetoed that idea, telling him to use three very young dancers in the company: Stacy Caddell, Susan Gluck, and Roma Sosenko. Mr. Martins says, "I can only guess at what he intended: perhaps to keep the work young and sweet, to strengthen my ties to the company's young members, or perhaps just not to waste his ballerinas?"[28]

• George Balanchine knew what he wanted, and he knew how to describe (and often to demonstrate) what he wanted. While choreographing *Scotch Symphony*, he told his dancers that he wanted them to form a rhombus—a word that everybody paid attention to. Allegra Kent writes in *Once a Dancer …*, "Everyone had perked up at the unusual word. What had interested me was his precision and exactness. Any old parallelogram would not do. He wanted an equilateral parallelogram."[29]

• Jerome Robbins was a perfectionist. When he was helping The New York City Ballet get ready to perform his *West Side Story*, he made changes to the end of the "Cool" dance, adding a knee slide and taking out some steps. At one point, he turned to choreographer Alan Johnson and said, "Maybe after 40 years I'll get it right." Mr. Johnson was amazed, and he said in an interview later, "While we all thought it was perfect, he thought it could be better."[30]

Christmas

• For Christmas one year, movie star Rock Hudson gave away stock. He gave friends one share of stock in a publically traded company that had something to do with the gift recipient's life. Opera soprano Marilyn Horne and her husband, conductor Henry Lewis, each got a share of stock in an airline company because they traveled so much and so often. Their very young child, Angela, got a share of stock in a baby-food company.[31]

Clothing

• According to rumor, gay actor Ernest Thesiger always wore a string of pearls around his neck. At the beginning of World War II, while he was in Oxford, the air raid siren went off, and he went to an air raid shelter where he attracted a lot of attention because of his clothing — Russian high-necked pajamas and a truly spectacular dressing gown — and because he was busily engaging in his hobby of needlework. Soon, the other people in the shelter began to sleep, and Mr. Thesiger knew that he wasn't attracting as much attention as before — so he grabbed his throat and shouted, "My God! My pearls! No, no, it's all right. I've got them on." Another person who wore clothes well was Dame Marie Tempest, who always looked good on stage. When she was dressed for a role, she always stood and never sat in her dressing room so that the costume stayed fresh. Once, an actress who was often late for work flung herself down before Dame Marie to ask for forgiveness, but Dame Marie ordered her, "Get up! Get up! Have you no respect for your management's clothes?"[32]

• Enrico Caruso and Frances Alda met on a ferryboat to travel together to and make some recordings in Camden, New Jersey. It was a rainy day, and Mr. Caruso pointed out to Ms. Alda, "You have no rubbers [rainy-day footwear] on." Ms. Alda replied, "I don't like to wear rubbers. I have pretty feet, and I'm proud of them. I'm a woman." Mr. Caruso was still worried about her, and once they were in Camden, he took Ms. Alda to the best shoe store there and had the employees bring a large assortment of rainy-day footwear until Ms. Alda found a pair she liked. Only then did they make the recordings.[33]

• Many people know very little about the personal lives of ballerinas and see them only on stage dressed in tutus. In January 1934, after Anton Dolin and Alicia Markova had made ballet history by being the first two British artists to dance the lead roles in *Giselle*, they decided to relax by going to a movie. At the movie theater, two young women saw them. One young woman nudged the other, and said, "Look, there's Markova!" The other woman looked and then said, "It can't be. She's wearing a blouse and skirt."[34]

Composers

• The French composer Camille Saint-Saëns had his eccentricities. Opera singer Nellie Melba picked him up in her carriage to take him to a party, but he suddenly said that he had to go back to his house. Although it meant that they would be late for the party, they went back, and he entered his house and then returned. When Ms. Melba asked what he had forgotten, Mr. Saint-Saëns replied, "My toothbrush. I have no key. I find, from long practice, that my toothbrush opens the door. So I always carry it with me." Ms. Melba wrote in her autobiography, *Melodies and Memories*, "He was one of the few men I have met who never made the faintest attempt to be agreeable to people for whom he did not care." A woman once tried to get him to dine at her home—"*Cher Maître*, will you not dine with me next week?"—but he declined, saying that he had no time. She insisted, "But could you not be *very* nice, just for me?" He told her, "I don't want to be nice to you." Once, Mr. Saint-Saëns visited Ms. Melba at her home. The footman was late in announcing his presence, so Mr. Saint-Saëns started playing Ms. Melba's piano fortissimo to get her attention. It worked. By the way, one of the parties given by dancer Isadora Duncan ended on a Nile houseboat—after starting in Paris and then moving on to Venice.[35]

• As a young man, Arturo Toscanini was able to meet Giuseppe Verdi and go over the score for Verdi's *Four Sacred Pieces*. Before their meeting, Toscanini studied the score carefully and was very puzzled over a passage. When he met Verdi, Toscanini played the passage, slowing down despite a temptation to maintain the tempo. Verdi was very pleased and slapped him on the back, saying "Bravo!" Toscanini replied, "But, Maestro, you don't know what anguish that place has caused me. You gave no indication of a retard." Verdi replied, "And can you imagine what some asses of conductors would make of it if I *had* marked a retard?"[36]

• Igor Stravinsky lived in the days before trifocals. According to opera soprano Marilyn Horne, he wore three pairs of eyeglasses: one on his nose, one on his forehead, and one on the top of his head. He would switch his eyeglasses so he could see whatever it was he wanted to look at. Ms. Horne attended lectures on music given by Aldous Huxley. She remembers that he loved the word "extraordinary." In one lecture, he used that word 50 times—his record. After one of her early auditions, an agent said about her, "*Die kleine Dicke wird etwas sein*," which means, "That little fat one is going places!"[37]

Conductors

• Walter Damrosch once conducted the New York Philharmonic in his own *Cyrano de Bergerac*. Unfortunately, some audience members started leaving early. Noticing this, Mr. Damrosch addressed the members of the audience after the end of Act 2: "Please don't go home yet—the best part of the opera is coming." The audience stayed in their seats, and at the end of the opera applauded vigorously. By the way, Sir Thomas Beecham definitely had his opera scores memorized, although he might forget other things. At Birmingham, where he was a guest conductor, he calmly smoked a cigarette before a performance, then as he walked to the podium to conduct, he asked the theater manager, "By the way, what opera are we playing tonight?"[38]

• Horn player Harold Meek often heard Aaron Copland say to conductor Serge Koussevitzky during rehearsals, "It sounds better that way. I will change it in my score." The composer Gretchaninoff once objected to a change Maestro Koussevitzky was making in a premiere of some of his music, but Maestro Koussevitzky told the orchestra, "Don't pay any attention to him. He is an old man and doesn't know what he wants." Béla Bartók, however, declined to change his music in any way for Maestro Koussevitzky.[39]

• Conductor Arturo Toscanini failed to get the vocal effects he wanted while rehearsing a soprano with two prominent frontal developments. Finally, he grew so frustrated that he jumped on stage, grabbed the soprano's two enormous talents, and shouted, "If only these were brains!" Maestro Toscanini hated the fascist Benito Mussolini and what he was doing to Italy. When Mr. Toscanini learned that a top aide of fascist General Francisco Franco had died in a plane crash, he shouted, "But Mussolini, he keeps on flying. Nothing kills him."[40]

• Not all singers and musicians are as good as we would like to be: 1) A singer once came to Sir Thomas Beecham for advice about his son. He explained that his son was going to Oxford, but still didn't know what he wanted to do with his life. He wasn't interested in law or politics, and his family didn't want him to go into business. Sir Thomas asked, "Why not make a singer of him?" The singer explained that this suggestion was quite impossible, as his son didn't have any kind of voice. "Ah, I see," joked Sir Thomas. "A family failing." 2) Giacomo Puccini, the composer of *Madame Butterfly*, was once upset to hear an organ-grinder on the street play some of his music at the wrong tempo, so he showed him how to play the music correctly. The next day he saw the organ-grinder again and noticed that he was proudly displaying a new sign: "Pupil of Puccini." 3) Rutland Barrington, despite not being a particularly good singer, created many comedy roles in Gilbert and Sullivan comic operas. During the opening night for *Patience*, one of Sir William Schwenck Gilbert's friends said to him, "Barrington's in good voice. He's singing in tune." "Yes," replied Sir William, "opening night nerves."[41]

• For a while, Ludwig van Beethoven was both a pianist and a conductor, conducting when he wasn't playing at a concert, and vice versa. According to Ignaz von Seyfried, Beethoven's page turner at an 1803 concert, Beethoven sometimes became excited by the music, and he conducted much too quickly for the orchestra to keep up. At those times, the first violinist would stand up and conduct properly—the orchestra watched him instead of Beethoven.[42]

• Conductor Arturo Toscanini liked fast cars. When he was riding with a friend who was shocked by how fast the car was going, he would say that the car was going "adagio" (slow), and then he would request his chauffeur to speed up. At La Scala, early in his career, Maestro Toscanini was so offended by a musician that he threw his baton at him and injured his eye. The musician sued, and the Maestro was forced to pay damages.[43]

• Here are two short anecdotes about conductors: 1) At six years of age, the future Sir Thomas Beecham heard a concert of music by Edvard Grieg. Late that night, he got out of bed, went into his parents' bedroom, and requested piano lessons. 2) While living in the small town of Hancock, Maine, conductor Pierre Monteux gave it a fire engine—and a fire station to house the fire engine.[44]

• Fritz Reiner was known for conducting with such a tiny beat that many musicians had great difficulty seeing it to follow it. Once, at a rehearsal with the San Francisco Opera, the bass clarinetist nodded. Thinking that the musician had fallen asleep, Mr. Reiner called out, "Mr. Fragali, do you know where you are?" Mr. Fragali answered, "No, I'm sorry, Maestro. I'm lost, too."[45]

- During a rehearsal, Sir Hamilton Harty urged a trumpet player to blow softer and softer. The trumpet player objected, "But, Sir Hamilton, it's marked *forte*." Sir Hamilton replied, "Well, make it twenty." After a concert, someone asked oboist Alec Whittaker who had been the conductor. Mr. Whittaker replied, "I don't know. I didn't look."[46]

Costumes

- Tutus are beautiful, but they can create mishaps. Isabel McMeekan, a first soloist at the Royal Ballet, once went into a deep back bend. Unfortunately, her tiara got caught onto her tutu. She says, I was absolutely stuck, until my partner realized what had happened and wrenched me free." When Royal Ballet principal dancer Lauren Cuthbertson debuted in *Swan Lake*, her tutu was both brand-new and very stiff. She remembers, "I was trying to make my first entrance as silent and soft as possible, and I could hear my tutu making this crunching sound, like a bowl of Rice Krispies." Still, tutus have advantages. According to Ms. McMeekan, "Obviously, it makes me feel glamorous and feminine, but it also affects the way I work, the articulation of the port de bras and legs. I like the feeling of being very corseted by the bodice, and being very conscious of the angle of the skirt. When you're on stage with all that sparkle, it heightens everything."[47]

- While appearing in the *Greenwich Village Follies* early in her career, modern dance pioneer Martha Graham's solos stopped the show each night; however, the stage manager was still not satisfied. He insisted that Ms. Graham appear on stage with the other dancers, wearing a fancy, low-cut gown. The gown disgusted Ms. Graham, and she declined to wear it. Therefore, the stage manager gave her an ultimatum: Either wear the gown, or have your solos cut from the show. Ms. Graham pointed out that her solos were the audience's favorite part of the show, and she still declined to wear the gown. Her solos were cut, but only for a short time. The show was much weaker without her solos, so the stage manager quickly restored them and stopped requesting that she wear the gown.[48]

• Things sometimes get hectic when a dance troupe travels constantly and performs at many different theaters, some of which have the dressing rooms a couple of stories above the stage, making quick changes difficult. While Anna Pavlova's dance troupe was performing at one theater, a dance ended and another dancer named Jean took her place behind the curtain. Suddenly, someone yelled, "Quick! Jean's forgot her pants for *Greek*!" The pants were thrown down from upstairs, and Jean caught them just as the curtain began to rise.[49]

• In 1949, Alicia Alonso and her dance troupe, Ballet Alicia Alonso, toured South America, where they sometimes endured financial distress. Once, Ms. Alonso needed a costume so she could dance *The Dying Swan*, so her mother made a costume out of a pair of curtains from their hotel.[50]

Chapter 2: From Critics to Food

Critics

- Critics vary greatly: 1) Some are very critical: Carl Gaertner once attended a recital in which Remenyi, a famous Hungarian violinist, played Bach. Mr. Gaertner hissed during the performance, so Mr. Remenyi asked his critic to identify himself. Mr. Gaertner rose and said, "You play Bach like a fool." Mr. Remenyi remained calm, and merely said, "Perhaps so, but will my critic show me how *not* to play Bach like a fool?" Mr. Gaertner did not rise to the challenge, but simply left—to the laughs of the other members of the audience. 2) Music teachers can be good critics: As a young woman, opera singer Marie Tempest had a 19-inch waist—the result of stuffing her body into a tight corset, as was the custom in her day. She auditioned for the famous voice teacher Manuel Garcia, who listened to her and then told her, "Thank you. Will you please go home at once, take off that dress, rip off those stays, and let your waist out to at least 25 inches. When you have done so, you may come back and sing to me, and I will tell you whether you have any voice." Ms. Tempest later said, "He was quite right. No one can sing when laced in as tightly as I was. I went home, and I've never had a 19-inch waist since." 3) Some societies are not good critics: Show business has not always been regarded as a respectable career. The famous coloratura soprano Luisa Tetrazzini and her sister once stayed early in her career in humble rooms, the landlady of which was very kind to her. They thanked their landlady for her kindness, and the landlady astonished them by saying, "That's all right, my dears. I'm always good to theatricals, for I never know what my own children may come to."[51]

- Despite being a world-famous operatic tenor, Leo Slezak once spent a short time on the music hall stage and enjoyed it very much. (Music halls are places of popular entertainment, including dog shows, comedy acts, singers, etc.) Once a hotel chambermaid asked for a couple of free tickets for her and her boyfriend, which he readily provided. The next day, he asked her how she had enjoyed his performance, and she went on and on about his dancing dog and how she couldn't understand how he had taught the dog so many tricks. Mr. Slezak realized, of course, that she had confused him with the man who had the dog act, so he asked what she had thought of the opera star on the same bill. "Oh," she said, "I didn't listen to him much—he seemed a bit wet." By the way, bootblacks—people who used to shine your shoes when that was fashionable—sometimes had a sarcastic wit. Mr. Slezak used to tell this story: A man with dilapidated shoes once sat down for a shoeshine, and the bootblack—an Italian—gestured toward the man's feet and asked, "Excellenca, do you wish to have your shoes cleaned or your toenails cut?"[52]

- *New York Evening Post* music critic Henry T. Finck was outraged one day when he read a review of a musical performance. He demanded to know who had altered the words he had written earlier. He complained that after 35 years of writing reviews of musical performances that he should be treated with more respect. Everyone was puzzled by this outburst, and someone brought the original copy that Mr. Finck had previously written to show that no one had altered his words. Mr. Finck then looked more closely at the newspaper with the review and discovered that he was reading the wrong newspaper—the *New York Globe*—and a rival critic had written the review. According to eyewitnesses, Mr. Finck was not drunk when this happened. Also according to eyewitnesses, Mr. Finck exited the scene—amid the laughter of his colleagues—quickly.[53]

- Even a bad review can be helpful in advancing a career. When Paul Taylor choreographed and performed *7 New Dances* in 1957, the audience walked out after 10 minutes. Martha Graham, whose dance troupe Mr. Taylor had been in, even told him, "You naughty boy." And in a famous review, Louis Horst simply put his name at the bottom of a blank page. Of course, Mr. Taylor was bothered by these reactions—but the review had good results. He says, "I was disappointed and mad that people didn't understand what I had done. But that review was a big help because it brought me great notoriety. No one had heard of Paul Taylor before that."[54]

• Following a performance of *Scotch Symphony*, in which Maria Tallchief was tossed in the air and then caught by André Eglevsky, two great ballerinas—Alicia Markova and Alexandra "Choura" Danilova—visited her and complimented her backstage. However, Ms. Danilova had a piece of advice: "But, you know, dear, when you're thrown in the air, back must be arched, head must be up high. Must be unconcerned." Ms. Tallchief explained, "Well, yes, Choura, I know. I'm trying to be serene, but I'm scared to death André's not going to catch me. Four of those boys are tossing me, and he's got to catch me all by himself."[55]

• Austrian pianist Artur Schnabel once made an excellent criticism at a rehearsal, saying to a conductor, "You are there and I am here. But where is Beethoven?" The conductor took the criticism to heart and thereafter did things Mr. Schnabel's—and Beethoven's—way. As conductor of the Philadelphia Orchestra, Leopold Stokowsky was infuriated by stragglers arriving late to his concerts. To make a point, he once had the musicians in his orchestra straggle in, individually and in twos, long after the concert was scheduled to start.[56]

• The Peruvian contralto Marguerite D'Alvarez had the misfortune of slipping on some steps in Chicago while singing the role of Delilah. Even more unfortunate for Ms. D'Alvarez was the presence in the audience of Mary Garden—who exclaimed, "My God, she's making her entrance into the Chicago Opera like Balaam into Jerusalem." This remark quickly made the rounds of the opera critics, and quickly Ms. D'ALvarez decided to leave Chicago. (And even quicker Ms. D'Alvarez and Ms. Garden became enemies.)[57]

• Creative people suffer ups and downs in their work, but sometimes a creation that at first is rejected is later recognized as a classic—and, of course, sometimes a creator will rework and improve an earlier creation. Someone said to choreographer George Balanchine, "Your last two or three ballets have not been very successful. What do you have to say about that?" Mr. Balanchine replied, "Give me some time, and maybe they'll be masterpieces."[58]

• Some singers are true artists. At age 16, Brazilian pianist Guiomar Novaes competed in a contest at the Paris Conservatory and won first prize: a grand piano. The judges were forced to listen to the same pieces that were played over and over again by many, many pianists. You would expect the judges to get tired of the music; however, they asked Ms. Novaes to play Schumann's *Etudes Symphoniques* a second time—simply because they enjoyed her playing so much.[59]

• Mrs. Patrick Campbell was very capable of being insulting when she disliked something, even while on stage. During the famous screen scene in Sheridan's *School for Scandal*, Mrs. Campbell felt that Fred Terry and William Farren were acting too slowly. Despite being on stage behind the screen in the role of Mrs. Teazle, Mrs. Campbell suddenly shouted, "Oh, do get on, you old pongers!"[60]

• Lotte Lehmann once sang an opera in Vienna before the head of a duchy. After the opera, she waited eagerly to hear what he had thought about her performance, but he only wagged his finger at her and said, "I watched you in the second act when you sat with your head resting on the gentleman's knee, to see if you would move. … It was very good but you wriggled once." By the way, some singers used to have fun in *Die Walküre* when Sieglinde served food to Hunding and Siegmund. While performing in London, Otto Helgers of the Berlin Opera, who played Hunding, used to say to Ms. Lehmann, who played Sieglinde, "What have you cooked today? I don't want always pork and beans."[61]

• Pianist Ignacy Paderewski once gave a performance in which everything had gone wrong. Rushing to leave the theater afterward, he hopped into a cab. The cab driver asked, "Where to?" In a hurry to be away from the theater, Paderewski replied, "Anywhere." The cab driver looked at Paderewski's bushy red hair and then said, "I'll take you to a barber."[62]

- A critic for the *New York Times* once accused tenor Michele Molese of producing "squeezed" top notes, so Mr. Molese sang a perfect top note at a performance, then stepped up to the footlights and announced to the audience, "That high C is for Mr. [Harold C.] Schonberg."[63]

Dance

- British dancer Sally Marie had to dance naked in *Dear Body*, a satire by Luca Silvestrini of people obsessed with working out to make their body beautiful. Intellectually, she had no problem with this. She said, "I'd been arguing for ages that we needed a greater variety of bodies and ages in dance. It felt like an important statement to be on stage showing my tits." In practice, she was terrified. She explained, "When you're in a sauna, it feels completely natural. But on stage, you're really exposed." Also, in practice, she was many pounds lighter when she stripped off on stage. Why? She said, "I'd been too frightened to eat." Ms. Marie does have good advice for anyone who will be dancing naked: "Try to avoid being naked in a photocall. Otherwise you will find pictures of yourself all over the national press and the internet. And they never go away. At run-throughs, keep your T-shirt on. It's amazing how many extra 'techs' show up when they think there may be some tits on show." When London-based choreographer Arthur Pita had to dance naked in his choreography of *Camp* after a cast member was injured, he immediately started doing squats and press-ups for a very good reason: vanity. He explained, "I really didn't want anything to be wobbling for the audience."[64]

- Early in Martha Graham's career as a pioneer of modern dance, some people had no idea what to make of her art. A friend once asked her, "Martha, dear, how long do you expect to keep up this dreadful dancing?" Ms. Graham replied, "As long as I have an audience." Actually, old age made her stop dancing. In 1969, at age 75, she gave her last performance as a dancer. However, she continued to create art in her choreography, although she bitterly missed dancing. When Ms. Graham was nearly 80 years old, dancer Tim Wengerd saw her crying bitterly in the dance studio. She explained that she had had a dream in which she was dancing, and then she had awakened and looked at her hands, which were badly crippled by arthritis. Knowing that she was incapable of ever dancing again, she had begun to cry.[65]

Death

• Maestro Arturo Toscanini once gave each member of his symphony orchestra a gold medal showing a likeness of himself. The members were very happy to get the medals, and many gave them to their wives, who attached the medals to bracelets and wore them proudly. Maestro Toscanini suffered from a few superstitions. Once, he had just finished conducting the New York Philharmonic when an admirer laid a floral wreath at his feet. Unfortunately, the Maestro associated floral wreaths with funerals, and he fled from the stage.[66]

• Rudolf Nureyev lived to dance. He ate raw beefsteak so he would have energy to dance, and once when the mother of ballerina Margot Fonteyn served chicken to him, he complained, "Chicken dinner, chicken performance." Near the end of his life, when he was dying of AIDS, he continued to dance, even with a catheter in his body and diapers around his loins. He once said—and he meant it, "When the lights are extinguished, I die."[67]

• One of the early significant works choreographed by modern dance pioneer Martha Graham was *Lamentation*, a dance about deep grief. During one performance, a woman in the audience cried loudly throughout its presentation, and then she went backstage and told Ms. Graham, "You will never know what you did for me tonight." The woman's young son had died recently, and she had been unable to cry until she saw *Lamentation*.[68]

• While in Chicago, opera singer Mary Garden was nearly killed by a wild-looking man. She was auctioning off box seats for a charity affair, when suddenly a revolver fell near her. She looked around and saw a police officer dragging the wild-looking man away. Later, Ms. Garden sent a friend to the jail to ask the man why he wanted to kill her, and he said, "She talks too much."[69]

• Hector Gray, an actor, visited his friend, ventriloquist Ray Scott, who was dying of throat cancer, on his deathbed. After the visit, Mr. Gray said, "Good night. I'll see you tomorrow." Mr. Scott replied, "Perhaps you will, but I won't be seeing you." Mr. Scott was right—he died during the night.[70]

• In 1929, tenor Giuseppe Anselmi, a major rival of Enrico Caruso, died. In his will, he left his heart—literally—to the city of Madrid, where he had enjoyed his greatest successes. In fact, his heart is preserved there.[71]

Dressing Rooms

• While touring in the ballet *A Midsummer Night's Dream*, Robert Helpmann and company put on a performance in a sports arena because the town lacked a good theater. Mr. Helpmann was given the umpires' room as his dressing room, but unfortunately it was badly lit. A friend visited him and saw him standing on a chair that he had placed on a table in order to be close to the sole light bulb hanging from the ceiling so that he could see to put on the elaborate makeup that his role required. The friend asked, "Are you all right?" Mr. Helpmann replied, "Oh, yes, I'm fine, but heaven knows how these umpires manage."[72]

• Dancer Paul Szilard once hoped to meet David Lichine, ballet master of the Ballets Russes. Dance teacher Stanislas Idzikowsky agreed to introduce him, but as they were about to knock on Mr. Lichine's dressing room door, the door opened and Mr. Lichine's future wife, former baby ballerina Tatiana Riabouchinska, ran out as Mr. Lichine threw a toe shoe at her. Mr. Idzikowsky told Mr. Szilard, "I don't think this is the right time to introduce you."[73]

• Anna Pavlova and her dance troupe once performed in a theater in which the only way to go across the back of the stage behind the rear curtain was to go through the men's dressing room. When Ms. Pavlova was forced to go through the men's dressing room, she said, "I no look! I no look!"[74]

Education

• People need to be prepared in order to get a job—or take advantage of a big break. Balanchine ballerina Antonia Franceschi always told her students at the London Contemporary Dance School, "Listen, you're going to be auditioning. You've got to give me fifth [position], and you have to be able to work from there. Whether or not you use it all the time in your contemporary work, I'm telling you that you're not going to get a job unless you can give me a Balanchine fifth." What happens? She says, "They didn't quite believe me—but they found out later!" She remembers being an apprentice dancer for Mr. Balanchine and rehearsing *Ballo della Regina*. Mr. Balanchine noticed a dancer in the first row. He went over to her to see her dance, and he said, "No, dear, too slow." This could have been a big break for her, but she wasn't ready for it. Ms. Franceschi learned a lot from Mr. Balanchine. She says, "His attitude toward work has given me insights as to how to approach the next 45 years of my life. Do everything you want to do, and don't be ashamed about working hard to get what you want." Mr. Balanchine often gave advice. He once told ballerina Nanette Glushak, "Dear, I want you to be better than that girl next to you. I want you to think you are better than her."[75]

• Ballet students must know when to pay attention. Merrill Ashley remembers attending the first rehearsal for *Divertimento No. 15*. George Balanchine worked with the principal dancers and explained what he wanted in the ballet, but Ms. Ashley thought that those roles were beyond her and that she would be dancing a much more minor role, so she read a book instead of paying attention to Mr. Balanchine's comments. At the end of the rehearsal, she learned that she was supposed to be learning the role of one of the principal dancers. At first she was annoyed that she had been allowed to read a book instead of paying attention at the rehearsal, but then she realized that every time Mr. Balanchine said *anything* about dance, she ought to be paying attention.[76]

• Merrill Ashley and other young students at the School for American Ballet were excited and nervous when George Balanchine gave them a class. Of course, they wondered if they would be able to do what he wanted. Very quickly, they found out that they had a lot to learn. He looked at them when he entered the room and announced, "Nobody knows how to stand." Merrill thought, "We hadn't done anything, and we were wrong already!" Mr. Balanchine taught them how to stand before he began to teach them how to dance: "Chest out, shoulders back, head high. Look awake and alive."[77]

• When Maxim Beloserkovsky was a youth studying ballet in Ukraine before *perestroika*, he sometimes was able to watch bootlegged videos of such stars as Mikhail Baryshnikov who had defected from the Soviet Union. Because of the dancers' defections, students weren't supposed to watch these videos, but dance coaches sometimes showed a dance video of poor quality—because it had been copied so many times—to students and say, "Look how they do this movement." Young Maxim would go home and marvel, "My God, I just watched Baryshnikov!"[78]

• Near the end of his life, ballet great Rudolf Nureyev gave a series of dance lessons to his personal assistant, Simon "Blue" Robinson, while they were on his island of Li Galli. During one lesson, author Gore Vidal walked into the dance room. Mr. Robinson, embarrassed, said, "I'm afraid I haven't any talent, Mr. Vidal." However, Mr. Vidal assured him, "Don't worry. Many careers have been made like that."[79]

• Ballerina Maria Tallchief once watched master choreographer George Balanchine teach a class to 40 girls, most of whom had no talent for dancing. She told him later, "George, isn't it amazing that there's only one girl who's any good?" Mr. Balanchine's opinion was different from Ms. Tallchief's: "No, Maria. What's amazing is that there *is* one girl who's good."[80]

• As a child, African-American diva Grace Bumbry was very self-critical, often coming home despondent after a voice lesson. Often, her teacher, Kenneth Billups, would call her mother to tell her not to worry about her daughter's mood: "She's all right. She just had another voice lesson today."[81]

• Schuyler Chapin became general manager of the Metropolitan Opera. Earlier, he had studied with Nadia Boulanger, hoping to become a composer, but she told him, "My dear, you haven't any talent."[82]

Fans

• Enrico Caruso, widely regarded as the greatest tenor of his era, loved to joke. Once an autograph seeker asked for his signature. Looking through her autograph book, he saw a number of signatures, under which the autograph seeker had written such labels as "First among world's harpists" and "First mandolist of Italy." Mr. Caruso signed his name, then wrote under it, "Second tenor." While singing in Verdi's *La Forza del Destino*, tenor Enrico Caruso was supposed to throw a gun on the floor, at which time a stagehand would fire a blank offstage. Mr. Caruso did throw the gun on the floor, but there was no gunshot—so Mr. Caruso said loudly, "BANG."[83]

• At the height of his powers, tenor Mario de Candia cast a spell over the young women in his audience as he sang. While in a Paris salon, he performed a song whose last line was, "Come, love, with me into the woods." At the end of the song, a half-hypnotized young woman stood up and walked toward him, murmuring, "I am coming." Henriette Sontag, the nineteenth-century German soprano, was much beloved. In 1825, she sang in Göttingen in front of enthusiastic audiences. After she had left the city, the citizens of Göttingen decided that no other person was worthy of occupying her carriage, so they threw it into a river.[84]

- Opera fans really, really wanted to hear Enrico Caruso sing. On the days when he was scheduled to sing at the Metropolitan Opera, lines began to form very early, and no tickets would be left for those fans standing at the end of the line. Therefore, Mr. Caruso would often buy 100 tickets for standing admission, although these tickets were normally sold beginning at 30 minutes before the performance. (No one was going to say no to Mr. Caruso!) He would then take his 100 tickets, go to the end of the line, and start passing them out, saying, "Here—with Caruso's compliments. And I hope you enjoy!"[85]
- Opera singer Mary Garden occasionally could not resist having fun at fans' expense. After she had given a lecture during which she wore some fine jewels, a woman asked her, "Excuse me, Miss Garden, but are those the jewels the Czar gave you?" Ms. Garden replied, "Oh, just some of them"—but she had never even met the Czar. By the way, Ms. Garden used to play golf with her father in his old age. One day, he turned to her and asked, "Mary, would you get me a pair of very small opera glasses?" Surprised, she asked why he wanted them. He replied, "I can't see the flags anymore, Mary."[86]
- Even rock stars get older, but that doesn't necessarily mean that they stop rocking. It can mean that they acquire different kinds of audiences: the younger kids who want to dance in the aisles, and the older fans who want everyone to stay seated. Celebrity interviewer Will Harris' wife once danced in the aisles at a Tom Jones concert, and an old lady kicked her! And in Wales, a younger fan was dancing in the aisles, and an older woman wanted him to sit down. After a while, the younger fan told the older woman, "Excuse me, grandma, but would you please f**k off?"[87]
- English tenor Alfred Piccaver was greatly beloved in Vienna. After an October 1924 concert which Mr. Piccaver gave to the Viennese before departing for a season in Chicago, the audience refused to leave. Thinking to solve the problem, the hall manager turned out the lights and the hall electrician left the hall, carrying with

him the keys needed to turn on the lights. Nevertheless, the audience still refused to leave. Eventually, Mr. Piccaver satisfied the audience by borrowing a flashlight, going on stage, and singing seven encores. Then, and only then, did the audience leave.[88]

• Some opera fans can't afford the more expensive tickets that allow them to sit down, so they buy the cheaper tickets, stand for the first part of the opera, and then move into the seats of people who leave the opera early. On evenings when the opera is well attended and well enjoyed and audience members are sticking around for the entire opera, people who have bought the cheaper tickets sometimes complain—good-naturedly—during intermissions to their richer compatriots, "Why don't you people go home so we can sit down?"[89]

• During World War II, opera singer Helen Traubel offered her services to a Chicago servicemen's canteen. Of course, not everyone likes opera music, and she overheard a sailor groan and tell a friend, "Oh, no! Not more of that long-hair stuff!" Therefore, she told the audience, "I shall begin with a song by a composer who has made the peasants of my home town famous among music lovers all over the world"—then she turned torch singer and belted out the "St. Louis Blues."[90]

• Rudolf Nureyev very freely gave his autograph when asked, but he sometimes played a trick on the person asking for his autograph. Mr. Nureyev would hold out both the autograph and the autograph-seeker's pen, and if the autograph-seeker reached for the pen first, Mr. Nureyev, who felt that his autograph was more important, would pull the pen back out of reach, forcing the autograph-seeker to take the autograph first.[91]

• Three of the best violinists of all time were Jascha Heifetz, Mischa Elman, and Fritz Kreisler. Once, Jascha and Mischa were dining together when a waiter brought them a letter addressed to "The Greatest Violinist in the World." Both men were modest, but they wondered which violinist the letter was addressed to, so they opened the letter together and read, "Dear Mr. Kreisler ...."[92]

• Jazz drummer Max Roach was not always recognized in the United States, including the Harlem restaurant Sylvia's, where he regularly dined. Once, some Japanese tourists recognized him in Sylvia's and gave him a standing ovation. Seeing and hearing this, another Sylvia's regular customer said to him, "I didn't know you were somebody!"[93]

Fathers

• Leonard Bernstein's father, Sam, resisted Leonard's desire to forge a career in music, preferring instead that Leonard work in the family business. After Leonard became a world-famous composer and conductor, Sam was asked why he had opposed his son's musical ambitions. Sam replied, "How could I know that my son was going to grow up to become Leonard Bernstein?" In contrast, Leonard's mother, Jennie, supported her son's musical ambitions. When he was a boy who played the piano loudly at home, causing the neighbors to complain, she told the neighbors, "Someday you're going to pay to hear him!"[94]

• William de Mille, playwright of *The Woman* and *The Warrens of Virginia*, was the father of Agnes de Mille, choreographer of *Rodeo: The Courting at Burnt Ranch* and *Oklahoma!* However, as his daughter was growing up, he let her know that he did not approve of her trying to make a career in dance. One day, he asked her, "Do you honestly think, my daughter, that dancing has progressed since the time of the Greeks?" Agnes asked in reply, "Do you think you write any better than Euripides?" Her father answered, "No, my dear. But we have Euripides' plays. They have lasted. A dancer ceases to exist as soon as she sits down."[95]

• The father of dancer/choreographer Merce Cunningham influenced him greatly. His father believed that you should do what you wanted as long as you worked at it—in other words, don't just talk about doing it, but do it. (This is good advice—lots of people say that they want to be writers, but they don't write!)[96]

Food

• George Zoritch's mother was in France during World War II, but after the war she went to America to be with her famous dancer son. In New York, she met a friend of her son's because Mr. Zoritch was busy performing in Los Angeles. Mr. Zoritch was delighted with everything USAmerican, until her son's friend offered her a hot dog. Shocked, she replied, "During the War in Europe, when we were completely out of food, people would ever dare to eat dogs! Here we are in the land of plenty and you mean to tell me people eat dog meat!"[97]

• Wagnerian soprano Helen Traubel ate whatever she wanted before performing. Once, she ate ice cream and salted peanuts a few hours before performing. This shocked one of her tenor partners, Mario Chamlee, who worried that such a combination of food would produce voice-destroying mucus. Ms. Traubel sang well, as always, that night, and Mr. Chamlee exclaimed, "Exquisite! Give her nuts, give her ice cream, give her all she can eat! I may take up eating them myself!"[98]

• Anton Rubinstein once promised the orchestra he would invite them to supper if his new opera would be a success; unfortunately, at the opera's premiere, the audience made clear their dislike of it. Disgusted, Rubinstein went home and went to bed, but he was aroused later by a knocking at his door. He opened the door, only to see several members of the orchestra, who explained, "You invited us to supper if the opera was a success; *we* liked it very much."[99]

• When young Alicia Markova was dancing for Serge Diaghilev in the Ballets Russes, her governess would not allow her to eat chocolates, so fellow dancer Alexandra Danilova brought her some during morning rehearsals, but she would always tell her, "But if you no dance well, I bring you no more!"[100]

• As a choreographer, Agnes de Mille understood the appetites of dancers. Whenever she hosted a party at which dancers would attend, she always told her cook to make four times the amount of food she normally would. According to Ms. de Mille, dancers will even eat the pattern off the plate.[101]

• When ballet impresario Sol Hurok ate with ballerina Anna Pavlova for the first time, he was astonished by how much she ate and how she attacked her two-inch-thick steak. Following that meal, he ate many times with ballerinas and became accustomed to the vast quantities of food they consumed.[102]

• Modern dance pioneer Doris Humphrey did not worry about ordering in restaurants. She simply ordered whatever was listed fifth on the menu, then she would amuse herself at looking at the other diners and trying to guess their occupations from what they wore and how they acted.[103]

• Many people, including reporters, regard celebrities oddly. One reporter was so impressed by the dancing of Anna Pavlova that he told her that she must eat rose petals. Ms. Pavlova replied, "I prefer German cooking."[104]

Chapter 3: From Friends to Mishaps

Friends

• Leopold Godowsky Jr. (the son of the eminent pianist-composer) had twins. He once asked his sister to drive the three-year-olds home, adding, "By the way, please drive carefully as I have two violins worth $50,000 in the luggage compartment." His sister joked, "Which should I watch first: the twins or the fiddles?" Mr. Godowsky replied, "The twins, of course! The violins are insured." By the way, Moriz Rosenthal wanted to include one of Beethoven's last sonatas in a piano recital in Boston, although his manager wondered if the public would enjoy such a long work. Mr. Rosenthal joked, "I assure you that not more than 10 people in Boston can compose better music."[105]

• George Frideric Handel and Johann Mattheson were both composers and friends, although occasionally they had fights. Mattheson wrote the opera *Cleopatra*, in which he played Mark Antony. When he wasn't on stage, he played harpsichord in the orchestra pit, with Handel filling in while Mattheson was on stage. At a December 1704 performance, Handel was having so much fun playing the harpsichord that he refused to let Mattheson play it even after Antony had been killed on stage. Mattheson promptly challenged Handel to a duel; in the duel, Mattheson's sword broke on one of Handel's brass coat buttons, and Handel lived to compose his *Messiah*.[106]

• Loïe Fuller, a USAmerican dancer who became famous in Paris, once wrote the Curies, Marie and Pierre, for a sample of radium she could include in a dance. Madame Curie wrote back, explaining both the dangers and the cost of such a venture. The letter resulted in a friendship.[107]

Gifts

• Soprano Lilian Stiles-Allen, who was professionally known as Stiles-Allen because early in her career some organizers of concerts

disliked having long names on their programs, received several baskets of flowers after singing *Hiawatha* at the Albert Hall. Conductor Malcolm Sargent noticed that one basket seemed very heavy, and when Ms. Stiles-Allen looked at the basket closely she discovered that it contained two dressed ducks, green peas, and strawberries and cream! (Later, Ms. Stiles-Allen became the teacher of Julie Andrews.)[108]
• Robert Merrill sang opera at the Met in New York. In addition, he frequently sang "The Star-Spangled Banner" before New York Yankees home games. The Yankees gave him his own uniform, which sported No. 1 1/2.[109]

Good Deeds
• Often, one good deed leads to a good deed in return—and to a friendship. Ballerina Olga Spessivtzeva took lessons at the London school of Enrico Cecchetti, who of course had many young students who were fans of her and who hung around the dance studio so they could see her. One such student was Veronica Vassar, who felt ill during one class and left so she could lie down on a sofa in the dressing room. Ms. Spessivtzeva was in the dressing room, and she sprinkled some scent on a handkerchief and placed it on Veronica's forehead. She also gave young Veronica a tangerine to eat, saying, "Eat it—it is good for headaches." The next day Veronica did a good deed of her own by giving Ms. Spessivtzeva a small bunch of violets—her pocket money was limited and she could afford nothing else—and thanking her for taking care of her when she felt ill. Ms. Spessivtzeva asked Veronica to lunch, and they became friends.[110]
• As a very young man, Milt Hinton played bass with the All City Orchestra in Chicago. He and the band had just played their annual concert at Orchestra Hall when a very distinguished gentleman named Henry C. Lytton introduced himself to the bassists and said that he owned the downtown Hub department store. He said that he loved the bass and invited the bassists to visit his office in a few days. The bassists all went, and Mr. Lytton took the bassists to a room filled with

basses and invited them to try the basses. After leaving them alone with approximately 30 minutes, he asked if each of them had found a bass he liked. They all had, and Mr. Lytton said, "The bass you picked is yours for as long as you play bass. If you ever decide to give up playing, bring it back to where you got it."[111]

• Francesco von Mendelssohn was a rich man. Opera singer Nellie Melba once dined at his house and then sang. To thank her, Mr. Mendelssohn sent her a gift: a large, exquisite pearl that nested in a white satin box. In Paris, Ms. Melba took the pearl to a jeweler to have it set. The jeweler was impressed by the pearl and asked where she had acquired it, saying, "I am certain of one thing, however—it has not been on the market for years, or we should have known of its existence." Ms. Melba wrote Mr. Mendelssohn, who wrote back, "The pearl belonged to my mother. You must not thank me so much. I wished you to have something that belonged to her."[112]

• In 1980, at Cumberland High School, in Cumberland, Rhode Island, Aaron Fricke attended his prom with a man as his date, despite the opposition of the principal. After a lawsuit in which a judge ruled that Mr. Fricke could attend the prom with a male date, the two men showed up and had fun. Despite some earlier homophobia, including a punch that opened a cut below Mr. Fricke's eye, requiring five stitches to repair, the students supported him and his date at the prom. Late in the evening, when the song "Rock Lobster" was played, the students showed their support of Mr. Fricke and his date (and their support of fun) by dancing to the music—girls dancing with girls, and boys dancing with boys.[113]

Husbands and Wives

• Richard Strauss once worked with a temperamental singer named Pauline de Ahna. In a rehearsal in which she sang the role of Elizabeth in *Tännhauser*, she made a mistake and he criticized her. They quarreled, and she ran to her dressing room. He followed her, and angry shouts could be heard for a while and then silence. People wondered who had killed whom in the dressing room. Finally, a representative of the orchestra knocked on the dressing room door. Mr. Strauss opened the door, and the orchestra representative said to him, "The orchestra is so horrified by the incredibly shocking behavior of Fräulein de Ahna that they feel they owe it to their honored conductor Strauss to refuse in the future to play in any opera in which she might have a part." Mr. Strauss replied, "That hurts me very much, for I have just become engaged to Fräulein de Ahna." Pauline's temper tantrums continued after their marriage. Lotte Lehmann once had coffee and cakes with the Strausses in a garden. It rained, and Pauline berated her husband because of the rain. Ms. Lehmann said, "But, Pauline, how can your husband stop the rain?" Mr. Strauss said to Ms. Lehmann, Don't defend me—that always makes it much worse!"[114]

• Choreographer George Balanchine made a mistake when the Ballets Russe premiered his *Le Bal* in Monte Carlo—he neglected to send his then-wife, Choura Danilova, flowers. This meant that Ms. Danilova, despite dancing extremely well, was the only soloist not to receive flowers. Realizing his mistake, Ms. Balanchine sent her 100 roses the following evening—many more than she was able to carry home.[115]

• When ballerina Suzanne Farrell decided to marry dancer Paul Mejia, her mother was so upset that she called in a priest, Father Richard McCormick, to talk to her. Ms. Farrell and Father McCormick met, she revealed her feelings to him, and he asked her what she wanted to do. Ms. Farrell said, "I want to marry Paul," and Father McCormick replied, "Well, then, I think you should."[116]

Insults

• Soprano Kirsten Flagstad disliked receiving visitors backstage after her concerts and sometimes kept even very important people from visiting her there. Early in her career, she even declined to receive the great soprano Frances Alda. Big mistake. Ms. Alda was known for forcibly expressing her opinion, and she said of Ms. Flagstad, "Tell that

Norwegian peasant that her singing is great, but she had better learn how to dress her hair and put some polish on those rough nails!"[117]

• Helen Traubel, who was a somewhat large woman and a very fine singer, and Groucho Marx, who made many comic insults in his lifetime, once appeared in Gilbert and Sullivan's *Mikado* together. One day, Ms. Traubel arrived late for rehearsal and Groucho told her, "Hello, Helen, pull up a couple of chairs and sit down."[118]

Language

• When H. Algeranoff joined Anna Pavlova's dance troupe in 1921, he listened carefully to the other members of her troupe so that he could pick up a little of the Russian language. However, most of the other members of the troupe were from Poland, and so the words of "Russian" he picked up were actually Polish. He did eventually learn some Russian as well as some Polish, but he suffered a few mishaps along the way. Once, a Polish dancer named Nelle told him to say a few words to another Polish dancer who was going to bed. The words were a harmless rhyme and meant, "Good night, and fleas in your bed." However, as Nelle had planned, Mr. Algeranoff mispronounced a word, making the saying shocking. The Polish dancer blushed bright red, and Nelle danced with delight.[119]

• In his essay "A Ballet Master's Belief," which appeared in *Portrait of Mr. B*, Lincoln Kirstein wrote that George Balanchine could be blunt when bluntness was needed. For example, an overbearing stage mother asked him what he was going to do for her dancer son. Mr. Balanchine replied, "Nothing. Perhaps, only perhaps, he can do some little thing for himself." On another occasion, a young male dancer over-reacted to some temporary failure in his dance technique during a morning class, and he savagely bit his lip. Mr. Balanchine told the 17-year-old boy, "It is you who chose to be a dancer. I didn't choose for you."[120]

• At age 14, Canadian ballet dancer Olympia Dowd was given the opportunity to study and perform—in an international tour to Asia and Europe!—with the Moscow City Ballet. Also given the invitation was her fellow Canadian ballet dancer, 17-year-old Rebecca Blaney. Of course, precautions were taken. The men in the Moscow City Ballet were given a strict warning—if you flirt with the Canadian girls, you will be fired. Also, of course, the girls learned a few things they perhaps should not have learned—such as Russian swear words.[121]

• Impresario Sol Hurok once approached choreographer Michel Fokine for a synopsis of one of his ballets, intending to reproduce it on a program. Mr. Fokine said, "No synopsis is needed for my ballets. My ballets unfold their stories on the stage. There is never any doubt as to what they say."[122]

• One of George Balanchine's dancers was known as "Evil Annie" because she was gifted at swearing. The dancers with whom Ann Crowell Inglish shared a dressing room used to tape holy pictures to her mirror—but they didn't cure her habit of swearing.[123]

• Ballet shoes are handmade, and the people who make them are called makers. Once, before going to London to dance with the New York City Ballet, Patricia McBride remarked, "I hope so much to meet my maker while I'm there."[124]

Male Dancers

• When USAmerican dance pioneer Ted Shawn decided to make dancing his life's work, a fraternity brother in Denver tried to change his mind by telling him, "But, Ted, *men* don't dance." Later, he studied dance with Mrs. Mary Perry King. When he told her, "I shall become a great and internationally famous dancer with a style and technique of my own," she laughed. So, for the 25 years, whenever Mr. Shawn received good reviews for his dancing, he sent a copy to Mrs. King. (Finally, the two became friends.)[125]

• Talented female ballet dancers are common, but talented male ballet dancers are rare. When ballerina Alice Patelson was a child, her father told ballet choreographer George Balanchine that his two daughters were taking ballet lessons. Mr. Balanchine was unimpressed and told Mr. Patelson, "Too many girls; make boys." At the age of eight, Peter Martins accompanied his two sisters to an audition at the Royal Danish Ballet School. His sisters didn't pass the audition, but the young Mr. Martins was accepted into the school because boy ballet students were scarce.[126]

Mishaps

• Choreographer Merce Cunningham sometimes used the *I-Ching* to help him determine the order of movements in his dance creations. Therefore, dance writer Janet Lynn Roseman decided to use the *I-Ching* to help her decide which of her too-numerous questions to ask him in an interview. Mr. Cunningham was delighted that she had used the *I-Ching* and assured her that she had asked the right questions. By the way, when Mr. Cunningham was very ill, he went to his doctor, who soon cured him. Mr. Cunningham thanked him, but the doctor replied, "Don't thank me. Thank your parents for a good constitution."[127]

• Bad tenors are one kind of mishap. Gabrielli was a bad tenor in 18th century Italy. At the Teatro Argentina in Rome, after he had sung a few notes, the audience began hissing and shouting for him to get off the stage. Mr. Gabrielli responded, "You fancy you are mortifying me, by hooting me; you are grossly deceived. On the contrary, I applaud your judgment, for I solemnly declare to you that I never appeared on any stage without receiving the same treatment, and sometimes much worse." Mr. Gabrielli may have been too honest—he never sang there again. Of course, mishaps take other forms. For a 1980 production of Gasparo Spontini's *La Vestale* at the Wexford Festival, the set designer created a steeply raked (that is, steeply sloped) stage whose floor consisted of white plastic modified to resemble the marble floor of the Roman Forum. Of course, such a floor can be slippery, but care was taken to coat the floor with a non-skid substance to keep the singers from slipping. Unfortunately, on the final night of the production, the non-skid substance was forgotten. A tenor entered and slid into the footlights. Next the High Priestess in the play entered—and joined the tenor. Next came the soprano who had the title role. She had been warned about the problem and entered the stage cautiously, then left—while singing—to remove her shoes. This didn't solve the problem of slipperiness, so she left again—while still singing—to remove her tights. Her bare feet did solve the problem, but no one had warned the chorus about the slippery flooring. They walked on stage, and they slid to the footlights in a heap. By the way, many productions of Wagner's operas have a very dimly lit stage. Soprano Birgit Nilsson once threatened to wear a coal miner's helmet because the stage was so dark.[128]

• Mishaps are common in live performances: 1) John Julius, Viscount Norwich, once attended a performance of *Rigoletto* during which someone in the audience let loose a balloon. It rose to the ceiling, stayed there a while, then slowly began to lose altitude and drift to the stage, ruining the dramatic tension of the opera, of course, as the audience watched the balloon rather than the opera. Fortunately, before the balloon reached the stage, a member of the orchestra reached up and snared it with the mouthpiece of his bassoon. 2) In 1966, in London's Albert Hall, young ballet dancer Natalia Makarova fell down while performing *Giselle*. As she lay on the floor, her dance partner, Onoshko, pretended he was a referee in a boxing match and started counting, "One ... two ... three ...." 3) While dancing the lead in a production of *Swan Lake*, ballerina Cynthia Gregory caught her crown in some mesh that formed part of the scenery. Fortunately, after a few flaps of her swan wings, the crown came free. 3) At a 1956 performance of *Die Walküre* in London, Hans Hotter came on stage after donning an enormous cloak only to be startled by much laughter. He had forgotten to take the cloak off the coathanger and was wearing both the cloak and a fluffy, pink coathanger. Trouper that he was, he carried on.[129]

• Here are three opera mishaps: 1) Russian basso Fyodor Chaliapin not hesitate to boss opera stagehands around. In Massenet's *Don Quichotte*, he was supposed to enter the stage while riding a mule, which gave the stagehands an opportunity to get revenge. A stagehand stuck the mule with a sharp object, so Chaliapin rode a bucking mule onto the stage—he was barely able to keep his seat, let alone sing. 2) In opera, singers must be heard in the back rows of the opera house. Occasionally, this striving after volume results in a spray of saliva that can drench an innocent co-star. The tenor Pasquale Brignoli was known for his spraying. While on stage co-starring with Mr. Brignoli in Mozart's *Don Giovanni*, contralto Emily Lablache asked him loudly, "See here, my good friend, can't you for once spit on Donna Elvira's dress?" 3) Soprano Emma Calvé delighted in making the life of her co-stars in *Carmen* miserable. Occasionally, Ms. Calvé, playing Carmen, would put a flower in the mouth of the singer playing Don Jose just as he started to sing the Flower Song. She also would drop things on stage just so Don Jose would have to bend over to pick them up for her. One Don Jose, Jean de Reszke, absolutely refused to pick up anything for her despite the manner in which she cluttered the stage. He explained later, "If she thought I was going to bend down and split my elegant brand-new tights, she had better think again." At the end of the opera Don Jose murders Carmen. During one performance, after her character had been murdered, Ms. Calvé stood up and walked off stage to go to her dressing room. Mr. de Reszke, furious, followed her, then dragged her back to the stage, where he forced her to remain until after the curtain had come down.[130]

• Mishaps do happen in music: 1) Ferruccio Busoni once brought his own piano as he toured in Spain. This made him careless, as what could go wrong with the piano when it was his own piano? At a small town, he strode onto the stage to begin playing, but he could not — his piano was still in its packing case! 2) Accompanist Gerald Moore once had a page-turner who turned the pages much too slowly. When this happens, the accompanist is forced to nod to indicate that he or she wants the page turned. If the page-turner is slow, this nodding can go on for some time — sometimes to the amusement of the audience. After one movement of a violin sonata, Mr. Moore asked the page-turner quietly, "If you cannot read the music, why don't you turn the page when I nod my head?" The page-turner replied, "Because your head is bobbing up and down all the time!"[131]

• World-famous composer Sergei Rachmaninoff once made a grave error. Following one of Mr. Rachmaninoff's concerts, George Balanchine, then a mostly unknown choreographer, came backstage and told him, "I would very much like to choreograph a ballet to your beautiful concerto." Mr. Rachmaninoff became furious: "A ballet? To my music? Are you crazy?"—and he threw Mr. Balanchine out of his dressing room. Afterwards, whenever Mr. Rachmaninoff's name came up in conversation, Mr. Balanchine would say, "Lousy music." Instead of choreographing Mr. Rachmaninoff's music, Mr. Balanchine choreographed the music of Igor Stravinsky and many other composers.[132]

• Mishaps are common in the theater. 1) At the Haymarket Theatre, an old man called Bibby worked as the stage door keeper, but a better employee for the position should have been found. One night, the play was running late, so Bibby, who was tired of waiting, walked on stage, gave the keys to the lead actor, and told him to lock up when the play was over. 2) Michael Benthall once criticized the extras while directing a production of *Julius Caesar* at the Old Vic, saying that they weren't acting naturally. He told them, "Just behave as you would normally in a crowded street." That night, while a crowd of extras exited the stage, one of them called out, "Taxi!"[133]

• Robert Lindley was a famous 19th-century cellist. Once, he traveled in a stagecoach to play at Nottingham. The stagecoach capsized, passengers screamed amid the confusion — some passengers had broken bones because of the crash — and Mr. Lindley got his cello and played it to make sure that it had not been injured. This became a story that his grandchildren often asked to hear years later. By the way, Mr. Lindley could have been knighted, but he declined because being knighted would not make him a better cellist. (Also, he did not want to have to dress formally and wear a sword for the knighting ceremony.)[134]

• As a child growing up in Australia, critic Clive James and the other children were fond of eating Jaffas, a candy with a hard orange shell encircling a chocolate center. This candy was good not just for eating, but also for throwing. In Sydney, the Borovansky Ballet performed *Giselle* in a performance at which many children had brought their favorite candy. At one point, Albrecht lay motionless on the stage floor while waiting for Giselle. Unfortunately, his oversized codpiece made an inviting target, and a Jaffa sped its way directly on target. Albrecht left the stage left the stage earlier than he had intended—and in pain.[135]

• Elise Reiman really didn't want to dance in *Spellbound Child* because she had to carry two long, difficult-to-manage veiled poles; therefore, she tried to get off the stage earlier than her scheduled exit. The first time she tried, she found something blocking her exit, and when she tried again a little while later, she still found something her exit. When she finally got off the stage—at her scheduled exit—she discovered that the thing blocking her exit had been choreographer George Balanchine's foot. Ms. Reiman says, "He knew I didn't like the part, so he put his foot there and made me finish the choreography."[136]

• Whenever the Damrosch Opera Company performed in Boston, any extras it needed were played by students from Harvard University. The doorkeeper at the stage entrance got twenty-five cents for providing each extra, but he made much more money than that because he charged the extras fifty or more cents each for hearing the opera from on stage. This usually worked out well for everyone, but during a performance of *Lohengrin*, a Harvard student dressed in armor stood on stage and read the libretto of the opera—to help him see, he wore eyeglasses.[137]

• Balanchine ballerina Allegra Kent once had a "bad-hair" day while dancing in *The Cage*, a ballet by Jerome Robbins about a deadly insect—the praying mantis, which eats its own mate. Midway through the dance, her wig, which was like a black beetle, came loose, and in disgust she ripped it off her head, letting her own hair fall loose and wild on her shoulders. Ms. Kent felt unprofessional for not fastening the wig securely, but Mr. B came backstage beaming because he felt that the mishap had resulted in a better interpretation of the dance.[138]

• Joan Ehemann Stone had some good luck while dancing with Igor Youskevitch in 1956 with American Ballet Theatre in *Helen of Troy*. In the Prologue, a scrim got stuck, leaving most of the dancers behind the scrim. In front of the scrim was only Mr. Youskevitch, a star, and Ms. Stone, who was dancing the minor role of a lamb. With the audience's eyes on them alone, the two improvised a pas de deux. As you would expect, Ms. Stone marveled later, "What a great moment for me!"[139]

• While dancing the lead role of *The Prodigal Son*, Edward Villella used to slide off a table, one end of which had been lifted in the air by the drinking companions. During one performance, he felt a sharp pain in his back, and the pain continued after the performance. He didn't know what was causing the pain until a few days later when someone in his dressing room saw him without a shirt and told him, "My God! You've got a splinter in your back the size of a nail!"[140]

• The 32 fouettés—a fouetté is a spin with one leg on pointe while the other leg whips around—performed by Odile in *Swan Lake* are very difficult. When a very young Natalya Makarova danced with the Kirov Ballet in Leningrad, she had great difficulty completing the fouettés in her first performance as Odile. As she spun around, she began to move backward, and by fouetté number 16 she had completely disappeared into the back wing.[141]

• Sometimes getting the lighting right at an opera is difficult. For one of the operas in Wagner's Ring cycle, word was passed about the lighting from conductor Herbert von Karajan to his assistant, who passed it to the head of the lighting crew, who passed it to the man actually doing the relevant lighting. At one performance, the message was "More light on Wotan," but the man actually doing the lighting asked, "Who is Wotan?"[142]

• As usual, the dancers of the Robert Joffrey Ballet arrived on time for a performance at Greensboro, North Carolina. Not as usual, the crew of the Robert Joffrey Ballet went to Greensboro, *South* Carolina, instead. However, the show went on, and enroute to their next performance, the dancers celebrated a successful performance under less-than-optimal conditions by filling the water cooler not with water, but with champagne.[143]

• While singing Siegmund to Birgit Nilsson's Sieglinda in the first two performances of *Die Walküre* during the 1974-1975 season at the New York Metropolitan Opera, Jon Vickers withdrew the sword from the tree with such force that the sword flew from the handle and into the safety net protecting the orchestra. Afterward, Ms. Nilsson said that if she hadn't stepped back, she would have lost part of her nose.[144]

• Thomas Beecham once conducted the English opera *Dylan*. Of course, this meant that the English-speaking audience understood all its words. Unfortunately, this led to some unintentional humor. The hero came out singing, "I sing, I have sung, I can sing better." Since the hero was singing poorly that night, the audience found these lines hilarious.[145]

• Nora Kovach and her husband, Istvan Rabovsky, danced together and shared many experiences, including surviving the sinking of the *Andrea Doria* in 1956. When Ms. Kovach heard that photographers from *Life* were present to take shots of the rescue of the passengers, she ran to her soaked cabin, saying, "I have to put on my lipstick."[146]

- In Japan, while Nora Kaye was performing the 32 fouettés in *Swan Lake*, she noticed a disturbance in the theater, but she continued dancing. After she had finished the 32 fouettés, someone stopped her dancing and led her outside. As they passed through the exit, she saw that the theater was engulfed in flames.[147]

- Some opera singers can sing a part very well, but they don't look the part. Basso Luigi Lablache was a huge man; he stood six-foot-four and weighed 330 pounds. However, the audience laughed when he sang the role of a prisoner starving to death in a prison. His first words? "I'm starving."[148]

- Occasionally, one ballet may need to be substituted for another ballet because of such reasons as injury to a principal dancer. Margot Fonteyn was once amused to see this sign announcing the performance of a ballet: "*The Wise Virgins* (subject to alteration)."[149]

- In 1959, for a few friends, ballerina Tamara Karsavina acted out the mime scene of the mother in *Giselle* at a small dinner party in a London restaurant—and to the other diners she brought terror.[150]

Chapter 4: From Money to Problem-Solving

Money

• Here are two anecdotes that Colonel James H. Mapleson wrote in his autobiography: 1) While Mr. Mapleson and his opera troupe sailed to America to begin their first USAmerican tour in 1878, they decided to hold a charity concert for yellow fever sufferers in New Orleans. One USAmerican was very insistent in asking whether the money the troupe received would really make it to New Orleans. Reassured that it would, the USAmerican enthusiastically applauded and asked for an encore of every song—then donated only sixpence to charity. The total amount raised by the charity concert was £3 or £4—a very low sum. Insulted and embarrassed by the sum—and afraid that the media would find out about it—the troupe, which consisted of some of the greatest opera singers in the world, donated £20 apiece for the charity. 2) Sadly, the Italian tenor Mario Armandi, who was active at the end of the 19th century, was incompetent. He made his living by filling in all over Italy for competent tenors who were too ill to sing—he got contracts of one day in one city, a couple of days in another city, etc. Once, he got a contract for six days in a row in Naples, but soon after he began to sing, the opera-knowledgeable crowd began to hiss. After the hissing had reached an unbearable level, Mr. Armandi stopped singing, walked to the front of the stage, and raised his hand for silence. He then told the crowd that if they would stop hissing, he would leave Naples after the performance, but that if they continued to hiss, he would stay in Naples and honor the remaining days of his contract. Amused, the crowd applauded—and allowed him to stay for the rest of his contract.[151]

• Walter Legg, an English classical music producer, was kind to his recording artists. He was also persuasive — perhaps too persuasive. He once persuaded conductor Carlo Maria Giulini to agree to make a recording of Tchaikovsky's Fifth Symphony, although Mr. Giulini said that he had no sympathy for that piece of music. They started to record the symphony, but after 15 minutes, Mr. Giulini stopped and said, "I can't go on." Mr. Legge simply sent the orchestra home and did not try to persuade Mr. Giulini to continue. After Mr. Legge died, Mr. Giulini remembered, "And you know what a [financial] loss that is to a company. Then we took a long walk together in Hyde Park. We talked of other things." Of course, Mr. Legge could get angry. He had a collection of early recordings of opera singers and orchestras and violinists that his father had given to him when he was only 12 years old. When he was 62 years old, he offered to give his collection to what he called "a venerable Swiss institution," but the institution declined to accept it unless he also donated money as an endowment for a curator and for the maintenance of the collection. In a short memoir, Mr. Legge wrote, "In one of my better rages, I broke every record into bits and tossed the pieces into Lake Geneva."[152]

• Dancers sometimes make very little money—this was especially true before dancers started their own unions. In the days when elevators needed paid operators, a young dancer named Harriette Ann Gray wanted to join the modern dance company run by Doris Humphrey and Charles Weidman. However, Ms. Gray was dismayed to learn that she would make only approximately $100 a year and asked, "How do I live?" Mr. Weidman asked, "Do you know how to operate an elevator?" Ms. Gray answered, "No," and Mr. Weidman advised, "Then learn."[153]

• In his Foreword to *Portrait of Mr. B*, Peter Martins writes about George Balanchine's concern for not wasting energy (and money). One would think that the life of a world-famous choreographer is glamorous, but one of the things that Mr. B would do at the end of the day was to make sure that the lights of the main rehearsal hall were out and that the lights of the offices were out. Mr. B explained, "Con Ed is very expensive. If I don't turn off, lights will be on all night. Do you know how much you save if you turn lights off? Millions!"[154]

• Dan Siretta, choreographer of *Very Good Eddie, Going Up,* and *Whoopee!*, used his collection of ballroom material in his work. In 1979, the *New York Times* asked him where he got his ideas. He answered, "I have a lot of old dance magazines, theatre magazines, from the teens, the twenties. I do all my homework from this material. I'll go anywhere to find it and I'll buy anyone's collection." After the article appeared, people all around the United States contacted him about their collections. He spent a fortune because he would reply, "I don't want to look through it; just send it to me."[155]

• As artistic director of the Paris Opera Ballet in the 1980s, Rudolf Nureyev really shook things up, bringing in modern-dance choreographers and bringing in dance teachers who had not been taught in France. Once, Mr. Nureyev interrupted veteran dance teacher Michel Renault's class to make his own corrections. Mr. Renault objected, and Mr. Nureyev responded by breaking Mr. Renault's jaw. After Mr. Renault sued and was awarded 2,500 francs, Mr. Nureyev said, "If I'd known it would be that little, I'd have hit him a second time."[156]

• Florenz "Flo" Ziegfeld frequently needed money, although he produced many money-making spectaculars in his lifetime. One day, he telegraphed comedian Ed Wynn that he needed $5,000 immediately. Mr. Wynn thought that the money must be needed for an emergency, so he wired him the money, but Mr. Ziegfeld used all of the $5,000 for a luxurious private railroad car to carry him from New York to Hollywood in style.[157]

• Here are two anecdotes about money: 1) Good tenors are very well paid. After Cecilia Bartoli was criticized for driving around Rome in an old, battered Fait Topolino, she defended herself by saying, "I'm a mezzo-soprano, not a tenor." 2) Because of previous bad experiences, tenor Beniamino Gigli liked to be paid his fee in advance so he could put it in his back pocket and feel it once in a while on stage and be sure that it was safe.[158]

- According to Giuseppe Verdi, "An opera house exists to be filled." Once, the director of La Scala sent him a telegram saying that one of Verdi's operas had been performed there and was a huge success on opening night. Verdi telegrammed back, "Very nice, but please inform me of size of receipts at following performances."[159]
- The Marquis de Cuevas spent much of his wife's money on various ballet troupes. (His wife, Margaret Strong, was one of John D. Rockefeller's nieces.) He resorted to various devious ways to get money from her—once he even pretended to be ill and cabled her, "I'm dying! Please send $5,000!"[160]
- Sergei Denham, director of the Ballet Russe, tried hard to save money. One of his stratagems was to lower the curtain by 11:30 p.m. so that he did not have to pay overtime. Once, he dropped the curtain before the end of a dance, causing star dancer Igor Youskevitch to threaten to quit.[161]
- Tenor Galliano Masini once received a cable offering him 5,000 lira to sing in *Aida* in Verona. He sent back this telegram: "5000 OKAY FOR ACTS ONE AND TWO STOP FOR ACTS THREE AND FOUR LET'S NEGOTIATE STOP MASINA."[162]

Mothers

- When Savion Glover was a child, his mother, Yvette, a single parent with three children, used to ride a bus. The other passengers on the bus knew and liked her, and whenever she was late getting to the bus stop because of the time it took to get her children off to school, the other passengers would make the bus driver wait for her. Yvette took good care of her children. Savion became a renowned tap dancer at an early age, performing in the United States and in Europe. While visiting Monaco's Monte Carlo, Yvette and Savion came across a nude beach. She quickly took her son to a different location. While the young Savion was performing in *Black and Blue*, he hung out backstage with the older, long-established tap dancers. Their language was salty, but Yvette knew that Savion would learn much worth knowing by hanging out with his heroes (and getting some male authority figures in his life), so she didn't try to censor the language used backstage. Instead, she read her Bible, staying close enough to keep an eye on Savion but far enough away that she didn't hear the salty language.[163]

• Sixteen-year-old Isabella McGuire Mayes of Great Britain was one of the youngest foreign students ever to study at the Kirov's ballet school in Russia. Her mother sometimes visited her, but for much of the time she was without members of her family near her. Once, when her mother was visiting her, Isabella had a pain in her chest, so her mother wrote a note in Russian for Isabella's teacher. Unfortunately, being not overly familiar with Russian, she wrote that Isabella had a pain in her "chest of drawers."[164]

Names and Titles

• Albert Evans took over many of the roles danced by fellow African-American dancer Arthur Mitchell at the New York City Ballet, and many people were reminded of Mr. Mitchell when Mr. Evans danced. In fact, when Jerome Robbins was working with Mr. Evans on *Goldberg Variations*, he kept calling Mr. Evans "Arthur." When Mr. Evans told him, "My name is actually *Albert*," Mr. Robbins said, "OK," then immediately slipped and said, "Arthur, can you move over here?" Mr. Robbins never did break the habit of calling Mr. Evans "Arthur" because, he explained, "You move just like Arthur." This, of course, is quite a compliment.[165]

• Mick Jones, guitarist of the Clash, wrote a song titled "I'm So Bored with You" about his ex-girlfriend. However, Joe Strummer, singer of the Clash, misheard the title, thought it was a major attack on the United States, and said, "That's brilliant." They talked, and Mr. Jones discovered that Mr. Strummer had made a mistake. Mr. Jones explained, "No, no—it's about my girlfriend." Mr. Strummer replied, "Not anymore." The song became "I'm So Bored with the USA," a major attack on USAmerican cultural imperialism.[166]

• In 1931, Ninette de Valois created her biblical dance titled *Job*. However, because of censorship she had to change the name of the character "God" to "Job's Spiritual Self." At that time, depicting God on a stage was against British law. It's interesting to note that the writers of the Bible are against censorship. In their portraits of Biblical heroes, they included the warts as well as the good features.[167]

• Mid-1950s Metropolitan Opera conductor Fritz Stiedry loved cars. His Oldsmobile Super-88 even told him its name. According to Mr. Stiedry, "One night that car appeared to me in a dream. Above the radiator I saw a girl, a blonde beauty who said to me, 'Fritz, don't you know my name? I am called Philomela.'" From then on, Mr. Stiedry called the car Philomela.[168]

• In Rudolf Nureyev's production of *La Bayadere* is a dance named "Adagio with Gauze for Solor and Nikiya" in which the characters Solor and Nikiya dance while holding the opposite ends of a long white scarf. Some ballet fans have re-named this dance the "Toilet-Paper Variation."[169]

• One of the nice things that country and western singer Merle Haggard did for his wife, Theresa, was to petition the county to allow him to name after her a road that passed through his land. All along the road he put up signs with her name on them.[170]

• June Brae was one of the pioneer dancers of the Royal Ballet. Her real name was June Bear, but Ninette de Valois changed it because she didn't want anyone to refer to one of her dancers as a "dancing bear."[171]

New Year's Day

• On January 1, 1963, as 52-year-old ballerina Alicia Markova was in an airport before a trip to New York, a journalist asked her, "Do you have any New Year's Resolutions?" Without having thought about her answer in advance, she replied, "Yes. I don't think I shall ever dance in public again." Her New Year's Resolution made worldwide headlines.[172]

Opera

• Anton Rubinstein wrote several operas. He was very pleased by the rehearsals for one of his operas, and at the end of the final rehearsal, he announced to the orchestra, "Gentlemen, if my opera is a success, you must all come to my hotel after the performance for a champagne supper." The opera was not a success; in fact, the audience's reception of it was so bad that Mr. Rubenstein left after the second act and let someone else conduct the rest of his opera. But after the opera was finished, the double-bass player from the orchestra went to Mr. Rubenstein's home and said, "I have come for the champagne supper." Mr. Rubenstein said, "The opera was a ghastly failure." The double-bass player replied, "But *I* liked it." (Another version of this anecdote appears in anecdote #99.)[173]

• African-American diva Martina Arroyo got her big break when Birgit Nilsson became ill and was unable to star in *Aida* at the Metropolitan Opera. Ms. Arroyo said later, "When they announced that she wasn't going to sing, I think you could have stayed home, opened your windows and heard the groans. But audiences are for you—they want to see something happen." What they saw was the birth of a new star as Ms. Arroyo gave a superb performance. Ms. Arroyo married Emilio Poggioni, an Italian violist. The two maintained two homes: one in New York, and the other in Zurich, Switzerland. Once, the two were separated by the Atlantic Ocean, and each was lonely for the other. Therefore, they each decided to surprise the other, and each boarded an airplane. The next day, after arriving at their destinations, they were still separated by the Atlantic Ocean. Ms. Arroyo helped people as a social worker at the East End Welfare Center while she was studying voice. This led to a strange conversation after she won a top prize in one of the Metropolitan Opera's annual Auditions of the Air. A welfare recipient called her to congratulate her on winning the prize and then added, "I need some pants."[174]

- During World War II, Thomas Beecham hailed a taxi in New York and told the driver to take him to the Metropolitan Opera. The taxi driver said, "I'm sorry, sir, but we have gas rationing now, and the rules are that I'm not allowed to take passengers to a place of entertainment." Sir Thomas replied, "The Metropolitan Opera is not a place of entertainment but a place of penance."[175]

Parties
- Harold Bauer was a famous pianist, but he also played the violin. Fritz Kreisler was a famous violinist but also played the piano. The two sometimes performed at parties—with Mr. Bauer playing the violin while Mr. Kreisler played the piano. By the way, skilled flutist and composer Stephen Foster was wary of being invited to parties only so he could play the flute for the guests. After being invited to a party for that reason, he sent his flute to the party—and stayed home.[176]
- Belly dancer Fahtiem once performed as a surprise gift at a party for a garbage collector. His friends carried her into the party in a brand-new garbage can, but her entrance was unspectacular. As the garbage can had swung back and forth, she had gotten wedged in. When the can's lid was over, she was supposed to pop out. However, being completely stuck, she had to call for help—the partiers pried her out so she could dance.[177]

Police
- Ballerina Anna Pavlova greatly disliked Shanghai, China, after a disagreeable experience with a police officer. She had hired a rickshaw, but the owner demanded a little more than the usual rate, making so much noise that a police officer came over to investigate. The police officer listened to the rickshaw owner's comments impassively, then hit him viciously on the head and rendered him unconscious. After that, Ms. Pavlova stayed in her hotel room, except for when she had to perform. By the way, Ms. Pavlova used to have her photographs retouched so that her feet looked smaller than they really were.[178]

• After receiving an award from the City of New York (which allowed him to struggle for New York seasons for 25 years and forced him and his dance company to travel overseas for much of that time), Merce Cunningham told a story about composer John Cage. Because he was driving too fast, Mr. Cage was stopped by a police officer who told him that he was issuing him a citation. Mr. Cage said, "Thank you very much." After telling this story, Mr. Cunningham immediately told the presenters of the award, "And I thank *you* very much."[179]

• Christian Johannsen was from Sweden, but he went to Russia and became an influential teacher of ballet before the Revolution. Even during the bitter Russian winters, Mr. Johannsen wore only a light cotton jacket. Once, a policeman stopped him, then began to rub his nose with snow. Mr. Johannsen's nose had frozen, although he had not noticed it.[180]

Practical Jokes

• Robert Merrill was touring with the Met in *Aida* along with a chef-cum-makeup-artist named Poppa Senz. One day Poppa Senz told him to come to the theater before a performance, and he would cook him a spaghetti dinner. Mr. Merrill accepted the invitation, and Poppa Senz made a wonderful dinner with extra garlic. However, when Mr. Merrill walked on stage to make his entrance, the prima donna playing Aida smelled the garlic on his breath and slapped him—she was allergic to garlic, a fact well known to Poppa Senz. When Mr. Merrill looked over at Poppa Senz, who was standing offstage, he saw that Poppa Senz was doubled over with laughter.[181]

• Lieder singer Lotte Lehmann once wanted to sing in Hamburg, but the Vienna Court Theater, which had her under contract, would not let her. Finally, she became so angry that she raged away at Mr. Lion, the Vienna Court Opera secretary. He coolly picked up the telephone, repeated what Ms. Lehmann had said to him, then said, "What is that, your Excellency? I'm to send for a mental doctor and have Fraulein Lehmann taken away in a straitjacket?" Fortunately, Ms.

Lehmann noticed that Mr. Lion was pressing down on the receiver—he had not called anyone, but was merely playing a joke on her.[182]

Problem-Solving

• Creating dance involves creativity, effort, and problem-solving. Two examples: 1) Martha Graham often created the costumes for her dances, and sometimes she would decide shortly before a performance that the costumes were wrong, so she would rip them apart and resew them. Occasionally, there wasn't time to resew them, so her dancers performed in costumes that were fastened together with safety pins. 2) The dress rehearsal for *Primitive Mysteries* wasn't going well, although Martha Graham had worked on its choreography for over a year. Finally, she was ready to give up and take the dance off the program. Deeply frustrated, she screamed at her dancers, "That's enough! Get out of my sight! Go home! Go away!" Fortunately, music director Louis Horst told the dancers to stay, then he went to Ms. Graham's dressing room and talked to her. She then came out of her dressing room and began rehearsing again. On February 2, 1931, *Primitive Mysteries* debuted in New York's Craig Theater. The audience applauded so much that 23 curtain calls were needed, and critics acclaimed *Primitive Mysteries* a masterpiece.[183]

• When Edward Villella investigated the stage before dancing in Bangor, Maine, he discovered that the floor was too slick to dance on, so he called up a hardware store owner to bring some rock rosin. The hardware store owner didn't have rock rosin on hand, so he brought linoleum, thinking that it might be less slick than the floor. Unfortunately, the linoleum was even slicker than the floor. In desperation, Mr. Villella got some Coca-Cola syrup from the owner of a soda fountain and drizzled it on the floor. This made the floor sticky, and every time Mr. Villella raised a foot, a piece of linoleum came up with his foot. Therefore, Mr. Villella used a mop to evenly distribute the Coca-Cola syrup over the floor. During the performance, members of the audience could hear a sound "like pieces of Velcro being pulled apart" every time Mr. Villella raised his foot, but at least he didn't fall on stage.[184]

• Some people greatly respect music, and some people don't. 1) Franz Liszt once was disturbed by two women who talked while he was playing during a concert. He stopped playing, walked over to the women, and said to them, "Pray do not let me disturb your conversation by my playing." The two women stopped talking, Mr. Liszt returned to the piano, and he began playing again. 2) When opera singer Clara Doria was in Italy during the second half of the 19th century, tickets to the opera were inexpensive, and many working-class Italians attended many productions and knew opera well. Rosamond, Clara's sister who also sang opera, was practicing at home while an Italian workman repaired a lock. The Italian workman listened as he worked, and occasionally would nod and say, "*Bene, benissimo*!" This surprised Ms. Doria, but such scenes of evidence of working-class Italians' love and knowledge of opera repeated themselves and soon she grew accustomed to them.[185]

• Jazz musician Eddie Condon drank — a lot. His wife worried about his health, and so she gave him a list of jazz musicians — friends of theirs — who had died of liver trouble due to alcoholism. Mr. Condon studied the list and handed it back to her, saying, "There's a drummer missing." He did get seriously ill and ended up in the hospital. He was too ill to eat, and he was unable to take nourishment intravenously. One other route to get nourishment into his body was available, but Mr. Condon resisted using it because, he said, it lacked dignity. His doctor talked him into it by saying, "It'll make you feel better. It'll be like having a drink." Mr. Condon rolled over onto his stomach and said, "See what the boys in the back room will have." While ill, Mr. Condon received a blood transfusion and said, "This must be Fats Waller's blood. I'm getting high."[186]

• During his early years, operatic tenor Leo Slezak performed without some conveniences, but he always insisted on a private area where he could withdraw from the public while not singing. Occasionally, he was not given a private area but told to remain on stage in full view of the public between acts because the public liked to see a performer during private moments. In such cases, Mr. Slezak insisted on at least a screen to give him a little privacy. Occasionally, he got the screen only by protesting that he would not stay on the stage unless he were given a cage and was allowed to charge a fee to the public for seeing him in it. Mr. Slezak was a big man—six-foot-four and 300 pounds. Once, he sat on a chair on stage and shattered it. Later, he told the stage manager not to give him doll-house furniture, but instead to get him something more substantial. The stage manager promised that all future furniture for Mr. Slezak would come directly from the elephant house at the zoo.[187]

• Some amputees continue to make music. Paul Wittgenstein, an Austrian pianist, lost his right arm during World War I. He refused to quit playing the piano, and he began to transcribe a number of piano masterpieces so that they could be played with the left hand only. Eventually, he continued his career as a concert pianist, and composers such as Maurice Ravel created works especially for him. In addition, violinist Rudolph Kolisch suffered an accident after which part of the middle finger of his left hand had to be amputated, but he did not give up playing the violin. Instead, he reversed hands, using his left hand for bowing and his right hand for fingering the strings. Eventually, he founded the Kolisch Quartet.[188]

• Sometimes conductors can make mistakes. While conducting Dvorak's *New World Symphony*, Eugene Ormandy was displeased with the horns, so he asked first horn Anton Horner to rehearse them. Mr. Horner did, but at his own tempo, not Maestro Ormandy's. Afterward, Mr. Horner spoke to Maestro Ormandy, saying that the accelerando was in the music, and requesting that in conducting this passage, he follow the tempo established by the horns. Maestro Ormandy didn't want to do that, but Mr. Horner pointed out, "If you were accompanying a Heifetz or Horowitz, you would follow him. Just follow the horns." Maestro Ormandy did follow the horns, and the music sounded fine.[189]

• Vincenzo Bellini's opera *La Sonnambula* is about a sleepwalker. For the performance of the singer playing the sleepwalker to be effective, she must keep her eyes closed, but of course then she can't see to move around and walk to the bed on stage. At a 1963 production at La Scala in Milan, Maria Callas kept her eyes tightly shut yet walked directly to the bed on stage night after night. Opera expert Hugh Vickers asked Luchino Visconti how this was possible. The answer was that Ms. Callas was using her sense of smell on stage. She had complimented Mr. Visconti on a scent he wore, so he had doused a handkerchief with it and placed it on the bed.[190]

• Sometimes, music concerts take place in very cold halls. This can be a problem for singers who wear gowns. Gerald Moore once accompanied soprano Dora Labette in one of these very cold halls, and he noticed that "she sang like an angel and was a vision of loveliness in a diaphanous gown." Immediately after the concert, he asked her how she managed to stay warm in her gown. She lifted the skirt and showed him that underneath she was wearing corduroy trousers, whose legs she had pinned up so the audience could not see them.[191]

• While singing the title role of *L'Amico Fritz* by Pietro Mascagni in Savona, a small town in Italy, Irish tenor John McCormack realized that he was going to fluff the high B flat in "O amore, o bella luce del core." Fortunately, with great presence of mind, he opened his mouth wide, sang nothing, but acted as if he had sung the note perfectly. The audience heard only the loud orchestra and were fooled by Mr. McCormack's acting into thinking that they had heard the high B flat. They applauded Mr. McCormack—vigorously.[192]

• Giulio Gatti-Casazza had an interesting way of dealing with opera stars when he was General Manager of the Metropolitan Opera. For example, Olive Fremstad once complained that her roles were too heavy and so she wanted lighter roles. Mr. Gatti-Casazza therefore gave her the very light—and for her, undemanding—role of the courtesan Giulietta in Offenbach's *Tales of Hoffmann*. Very quickly, Ms. Fremstad found herself willing to undertake the heavier roles that Mr. Gatti-Casazza wanted her to undertake.[193]

• Composer/conductor Nicolas Slonimsky, who was born in St. Petersburg, Russia, once ran into a problem at the entrance of Sleepy Hollow Cemetery in Concord, Massachusetts, when he could not prove his identity to a suspicious official in 1942, when the United States was fighting World War II. However, Mr. Slonimsky told the police, "Take me to the public library, and I'll prove who I am." At the public library, Mr. Slonimsky showed the police page 329 of *Living Musicians* by David Ewen, on which page was a biography and sketch of Mr. Slonimsky.[194]

• Rita Moreno started dancing professionally when she was very young, and once in New York she was performing despite being under the legal age for performers in that city. Unfortunately, the club she was dancing in was raided. Fortunately, the owner of the club gave her a mink to wrap herself in and set a drink in front of her so that the police thought that she was older than she really was. Ms. Moreno once wore a necklace made out of teeth. When a reporter asked her about the necklace, she said that the teeth came from her old boyfriends.[195]

• Soprano Grace Moore once ran into a problem with a Polish tenor who continually upstaged her in *La Boheme*. One of his tricks was to take the chair that Mimi—Ms. Moore's character—was supposed to faint in and push it backstage, thus giving himself the front-and-center spot. This trickery so infuriated the stage crew that the second time the Polish tenor tried to pull this trick, he found that he could not push the chair backstage—the stage crew had nailed it to the floor.[196]

• Milton Cross was the announcer for the Metropolitan Opera radio broadcasts. His knowledge of opera came in handy occasionally when he was forced to speak without a script. On one occasion, while a boring financial report was being read at the Met, Mr. Cross had to fill a half-hour of air time without a script. He told the plot of the opera *Il Trovatore* and talked about such things as scenery and dressing rooms. The *New York Herald Tribune* praised his performance.[197]

• Janet Reed was very nervous before she danced in *Coppélia* at the San Francisco Opera House as a teenager. The curtain rose, she looked at a sea of faces, and panicked. Fortunately, she looked over at the stage manager, who nodded happily at her as if she were the best thing that had ever happened at the Opera House, and promptly she forgot her panic and began to dance.[198]

• Pianist Leopold de Meyer once was asked to play in a Sultan's Palace in Turkey. But because the piano's legs were so short—they had been cut off so the Sultan's wives could play while sitting down—he protested. However, the Sultan solved the problem by having three slaves use their backs to hold up the piano while Mr. Meyer played.[199]

• Being an opera singer seems to be a glamorous job, and it is, but not always. While rehearsing Donizetti's *Roberto Devereaux*, Beverly Sills gave Plácido Domingo a fake slap that was unconvincing, so they decided that she should slap him for real during performances. Mr. Domingo admits that the real slap hurt.[200]

• When ballet dancer Felia Doubrovska fled from her native Russia in 1920, she did so on skis. She and some other dancers went out on skis, as if they were enjoying themselves on a vacation and then crossed over into Finland.[201]

• Ballerina Marie Taglioni is given credit for inventing legwarmers. Worried that her leg muscles might cool down too quickly, she cut the arms off a sweater and pulled them over her legs.[202]

Chapter 5: From Publicity to Work

Publicity
• Theatrical impresario Florenz "Flo" Ziegfeld knew how to get publicity. One of his first stars was French singer Anna Held. Word leaked out to the newspapers that Mr. Ziegfeld was being sued because he had failed to pay his milk bill. Word also leaked out that Mr. Ziegfeld was buying so much milk that it took six cows to provide his daily order. Enterprising reporters investigated, and they heard that Ms. Held was taking baths in the milk! This provided much publicity that helped make French star Anna Held a star in the United States. Of course, this was just a publicity stunt. Ms. Held did not take baths in milk—doing that would have made her sticky! Mr. Ziegfeld did not buy that much milk, and he paid a milk dealer to sue him. Playwright Max Marcin had read about ancient Roman milk baths, and Mr. Ziegfeld paid him $250 for the idea of the publicity stunt.[203]

• When Ruth St. Denis was very old, she asked dance critic Walter Terry why a certain publication was always so kind in covering her activities. He investigated and discovered that an executive on the publication had had a romance with Miss Ruth long ago—a romance that Miss Ruth had totally forgotten but which the executive had never forgotten. Once, the executive approached Miss Ruth and Mr. Terry, and Mr. Terry just had time to whisper the name of the executive's publication and the reminding phrase "night in moonlight California." Miss Ruth looked into the executive's eyes and said, "It has been so long …." The favorable publicity continued.[204]

Rehearsals
• Choreographer George Balanchine valued imperfect excitement over correct boredom. In a rehearsal, he criticized a dancer, saying, "No! Not big enough, does not travel enough, feet come together too slowly in assemblé. Do again." The dancer tried again, with more energy, and Mr. Balanchine told her, "Better, but not good enough."

Again, the dancer tried, this time putting into the steps all the energy she had. She jumped into the air with her feet together in assemblé—and she landed on her rear end in front of Mr. Balanchine, who appreciated her energy and smiled and told her, "That's right. Now I see something."[205]

- Pierina Legnani was the creator of the role of the Swan Queen in *Swan Lake*. Before dancing the role, she had astonished Russian balletomanes by performing 32 consecutive fouettés—32 consecutive spins on pointe. She attempted to keep how to perform such a feat secret, but Russian ballerina Mathilde Kchessinska secretly spied on one of her rehearsals and discovered that Ms. Legnani was spotting—looking at a fixed point as long as possible during a spin, then whipping her head around to look at the spot again for as long as possible. Spotting helped her keep her balance and not grow dizzy.[206]

- Wolfgang Amadeus Mozart was dissatisfied with the way rehearsals for his opera *Don Giovanni* were going—the soprano playing Zerlina kept giving a very unconvincing scream when grabbed by the lecherous Don Giovanni. Finally, Mozart solved the problem by sneaking up behind the unwary soprano and grabbing her. After she gave a genuine scream, he said, "You see, Madame, that is the way an innocent young woman screams when her virtue is in danger."[207]

- A rehearsal of *The Bartered Bride* in Covent Garden with Sir Thomas Beecham went badly, with the maestro making remarks more cutting than the singers deserved. Fortunately, Austrian tenor Richard Tauber came to the rescue of the singers by saying, "I'm sorry, Sir Thomas, but we've been singing it wrong for so many years in Prague and Vienna that you can't expect us to get it right in only one rehearsal."[208]

- During a rehearsal, ballerina Darci Kistler once fell with a crash in front of master choreographer George Balanchine. She was very embarrassed, but later she learned that Mr. Balanchine is very forgiving of falls during rehearsals—falls show that the ballerina is working hard and not holding back.[209]

Rock Music

• Here are two anecdotes about women rockers: 1) Jill Sobule got a big break while she was busking in the street. A flute student had suggested that the two of them busk "for a goof." A man passing by heard them—Jill was singing her songs in public for the first time—and asked if they would play in his nightclub. At first they didn't believe him—"Yeah, right. What club?"—but the offer, and the nightclub, were real. Jill performed there for three months, dropped out of school, and became a professional musician. Her biggest hit—which is pre-Katy Perry—is "I Kissed a Girl." 2) June Millington, lead guitarist for Fanny, met Cris Williamson and played music with her. During one conversation, June enthusiastically quoted some graffiti that she had read in a women's restroom in Arkansas. Cris looked at her and said, "June, that's me. Those are my lyrics." June adds, "She loved it."[210]

• In 1980, Joan Jett received 23 rejection letters after sending out tapes that included "I Love Rock 'n' Rock," "Do You Want to Touch Me," and "Crimson and Clover"—three huge hits. The letters said, "No good songs here. You need a song search." Fortunately, Ms. Jett printed 5,000 copies of the record, sold them, printed 5,000 more copies and sold them, and eventually landed a recording deal. She wonders, "Do they just throw these tapes into a bin of music, 'cause they don't have time to listen? And if they do listen, it's kind of scary that someone could hear three top-ten hits and miss them."[211]

• Rejection comes in many forms. Damon Krukowski was once a member of a punk band called Speedy and the Castanets. The band participated in a Battle of the Bands contest and was voted last in every category, including "looks"! Fortunately, he later got more respect as a member of Galaxie 500 and of Magic Hour and as a member (with Naomi Yang) of Damon and Naomi.[212]

Segregation

• African-American singer Marion Anderson was a huge success in Europe before she became a success in the United States. One day, she visited composer Jean Sibelius, who hugged her and said, "My child, my roof is too low for you." Ms. Anderson lived during the time of segregation, and theaters were segregated horizontally—the whites had the better seats in the front, while the blacks had the worse seats in the back and in the balcony. Ms. Anderson was unable to stop segregation in the theaters in which she performed, but she did insist on vertical segregation—one side of the theater was for blacks, and the other half for whites. In their half of the theater, blacks could sit in the front row.[213]

• The great dancer Bill Robinson, aka Mr. Bojangles, worked for social justice during the Jim Crow days of the United States. He often danced at benefits. Whenever an all-white audience was expected at a benefit, he asked that blacks be allowed to attend. And whenever an all-black audience was expected at a benefit, he asked that whites be allowed to attend.[214]

Sopranos

• Soprano Frances Alda was backstage, getting ready to sing the role of Lady Harriet in the opera *Marta*. She was especially looking forward to singing, in English, the song "The Last Rose of Summer." Unfortunately, a thoughtless assistant conductor told her, "You know, Patti said that was the most difficult song in the world." Because Adelina Patti had been one of the greatest coloratura singers of the late 19th century, this announcement shook Ms. Alda's confidence, and it took many, many performances for her to sing the song as well as she had sung it before the thoughtless assistant conductor had spoken to her.[215]

• Soprano Marjorie Lawrence was superstitious and always insisted that a penny be given to her for good luck before each performance. A concert at Covent Gardens started late because no one backstage could find a penny to give to her—eventually, a penny was borrowed from the box office.[216]

Tap Dancing

• Brooklyn Dodger Frenchy Bordagaray was fun loving, and he was honest. During one game, Frenchy was on second with the bases loaded, and because he was feeling good he started dancing on the base. Suddenly, the opposing pitcher turned and fired a throw to second, and Frenchy was called out and started for the dugout. Dodger manager Casey Stengel stormed out of the dugout and headed toward the second-base umpire, but as he passed Frenchy, he asked if Frenchy thought he was out. Ever honest, Frenchy replied, "Yep." Casey made a weak protest of the call, then he returned to the dugout and asked Frenchy, "If you were on the bag, how could you be out?" Frenchy replied, "I was doing a tap dance. He must have tagged me between taps."[217]

• Tap dancer John Bubbles, who created the role of Sportin' Life in George Gershwin's *Porgy and Bess*, was very good at stealing the steps of other tap dancers. He would watch another dancer practice, and when he saw a step that he wanted to steal, he would say, "You lost the beat back there—now try that step again." The tap dancer would repeat the step a few times, giving Mr. Bubbles enough time to learn it. Then Mr. Bubbles would say, "You know, that reminds me of a step I used to do," and he would perform a variation of the step he had just stolen. Usually, the other tap dancer felt flattered by the great Mr. Bubbles' attention.[218]

• Tap dancer Fred Astaire was a *Password* nut. Once, when *Password* host Allen Ludden was vacationing in Europe, and staying as a guest with Mr. Astaire's sister, Adele, Mr. Astaire telephoned him (when long-distance was expensive) just to find out why a certain clue had been disallowed on *Password*.[219]

Tenors

• The first time Enrico Caruso sang in public, he was not a success. Since he had not known he would be called on to sang that night, he had drunk too much wine. However, the next night, the audience was dissatisfied with the tenor, so they called for "the little drunkard" to sing to them. This time, Mr. Caruso was a success, and the next morning photographers were sent to his home to take his photograph. Unfortunately, his only shirt had been sent out to be washed, so Mr. Caruso draped his bedspread around his shoulders, and that was the costume he was wearing in the photographs of him published in the local newspaper. Mr. Caruso supported the United States during World War I, buying many Liberty Bonds. Once, he even went to the office of "Big Bill" Edwards, a Collector of the Internal Revenue Department, and requested permission to pay his income tax several months early, saying, "If I wait, something might happen to me, then it would be hard to collect. Now I pay, then if something happens to me, the money belongs to the United States, and that is good."[220]

• The great tenor Franco Corelli feared having dry lips while performing, so he hid wet sponges on the stage and in his costume while performing. Often, when the audience saw him raise his hands to his face during a dramatic scene, Mr. Corelli was really wetting his lips with a sponge.[221]

Touring

• Life on tour can be tough; however, at least once comic singer Anna Russell received VIP treatment. Arriving in town for a concert, she was met by a man in a chauffeured limousine who took her to a fancy hotel suite. The man explained that the chauffer and limousine were at her disposal, and she could visit any of the expensive restaurants in the neighborhood and charge it to his booking agency. In addition, he explained that only domestic champagne had been put in her refrigerator and asked if that would be OK, which she said it would be. Later, she learned that she had been booked by people who normally handled rock concerts (but who wanted to upgrade their image), and that she was receiving the treatment normally accorded to rock stars. The booking agency was very pleased with her. Not only was Ms. Russell satisfied with domestic champagne, but she didn't break or steal anything at the hotel. In addition, she did not appear to be high on drugs.[222]

• Ruth St. Denis and Ted Shawn went on a strenuous cross-country dance tour with the Ziegfeld Follies in order to build Denishawn House, where they lived and taught dance classes. When Denishawn House was dedicated, Ms. St. Denis placed her hand on the building and prepared to make a statement. The people present expected a fancy statement with rhetorical flourishes, but instead she said simply, "Every brick a one-night stand." ("One-night stand" means "One performance in a city or town.")[223]

• While on tour, Merce Cunningham and his dancers stopped one icy winter at a truck stop near Chicago, where they got a map and drew a straight line to their destination—Oregon. A truck driver, after watching them draw the line, told them, "Are you crazy? The only way you'll get there is by going south through Arizona."[224]

• Being a ballet dancer does not necessarily mean leading a glamorous life. Alicia Markova, one of the greats, remembers while traveling with the Ballet Russe walking through a train and seeing a "forest of legs"—48 pairs of pink tights hanging up to dry.[225]

• Early in her career as choreographer, Twyla Tharp wanted to take her dancers on a European tour. Getting plane tickets for the dancers was easy. Ms. Tharp told her dancers, "Call your parents." The parents bought the plane tickets.[226]

Valentine's Day

• Glenn Allen Sims, an Alvin Ailey dancer, says that he lives by Mr. Ailey's motto: "Dance comes from the people, and it should be delivered back to the people." He enjoys people telling him after a performance, "That really moved me." Once, a woman who was unable to walk told him, "Watching you onstage, I was able to move in my imagination." By the way, Glenn became determined to take dance lessons when he was a 4th grader. A really cute dance teacher showed up at his school. She was so cute that for Valentine's Day Glenn and other boys gave her gifts although they were not (yet) in her class.[227]

War

• Following World War I, Ernestine Schumann-Heink was leery of singing German classical music. (She had sung to support the USAmerican troops during the war.) Even while singing in Japan, she was very careful of which songs she sang, so she left off the program all songs by German composers. However, the Empress of Japan looked over the program and was shocked by the lack of German composers, asking, "Why, what kind of a program is this?" Ms. Schumann-Heink started to mention the war, but the Empress of Japan said, very reasonably, "Music has nothing to do with *war*! Music should not be affected by war. So put in your classics, Brahms, Schubert, Beethoven, and make it an artistic, beautiful program—or there can be no concert." Ms. Schumann-Heink very happily put the requested German classics into her program. By the way, Johann Brahms was fond of hearing Ernestine Schumann-Heink sing *Carmen*. She often sang the role in Hamburg, and so, when Mr. Brahms visited that city, he would telegraph the opera house and ask it to schedule *Carmen* "with the Heink."[228]

• Anna Russell's father was a military officer who once got into trouble during World War I. He was working at a camp for recuperating soldiers who had been wounded. Some of the soldiers had healed and were about to be sent back into combat, but they protested that they had done their bit for the war effort. Ms. Russell's father disagreed, telling them, "You've never done your bit until you're dead." This even became the basis for a music hall song: "You've Never Done Your Bit Till You're Dead, Dead, Dead." Her grandfather must have been a stern old man. He used to write his sons who were attending military school and ask them questions such as "What lessons do you like best, second, and third best? Give reasons." He also gave his sons lots of advice such as, "Be sure to evacuate your bowels every morning after breakfast."[229]

• During World War II, the Vic Wells Ballet continued to dance, thus raising the morale of British citizens—and the citizens of other countries. In 1940, the ballet dancers toured the Netherlands, and on May 6, they performed in The Hague. Just four days later, German soldiers invaded the Netherlands, trapping the dancers in their hotel until they could escape—smuggled away from the Netherlands in the hold of a cargo boat. Actually, the British Foreign Office had learned that German soldiers would be invading the Netherlands. British authorities were afraid that if the ballet tour were cancelled, the Germans would be aware that British military intelligence knew about the coming invasion; therefore, they let the dance tour continue.[230]

• During World War II, Maria Callas' mother sheltered a couple of British officers for six weeks from the Germans and Italians who were then occupying Athens, Greece. Shortly after the officers left, some Italian soldiers arrived to search the Callas apartment—from which incriminating evidence had not yet been removed. Maria, then only 17 years old, saved the life of herself and her family by going to the piano and singing. The Italian soldiers were music lovers, so they listened to young Maria and forgot about searching the apartment. In addition, the next day they brought food as gifts for the Callas family and Maria once more sang for them. Also during World War II, some Greek singers, including the very young Maria Callas (who was chaperoned by her mother), were "asked" to sing before some music-loving Italian soldiers in Salonika. The series of concerts was successful, and afterward the singers were asked if they wanted to be paid in food or money. Good food was in short supply because of the war, so all the singers replied, "Food!" They came home well stocked in cheeses, hams, sausages, evaporated milk, and other good things.[231]

• During World War II, the British sent bands overseas to entertain the troops. English classical music producer Walter Legg heard the bands auditioning at Drury Lane Theatre for overseas tours, and he marveled at the intonation of the bands, which was flawless although the theatre was unheated and very cold — Mr. Legge recalled "near-Arctic conditions." He congratulated the conductors on the flawless intonations of their bands, and one conductor told him, "You would have no intonation problems if you had our authority to put any man who played out of tune on seven days latrine duty."[232]

Work

• Impresario James H. Mapleson had many interesting experiences in music: 1) Tenor Pietro Mongini was insulted because a tailor had made his costume too small. He threatened not to go on stage to sing, but impresario James H. Mapleson promised him that he would fire the tailor and force him, his wife, and his four children to starve. Mollified, Mr. Mongini performed, and the next day Colonel Mapleson secretly informed the tailor that he had a wife and four children (the tailor was actually single) and then fired him in front of Mr. Mongini. Horrified at what had happened and worried that he would be the cause of the tailor's family starving, Mr. Mongini begged Colonel Mapleson to re-hire the tailor, which of course he willingly did. 2) Prima donnas can be vigilant in the pursuit of what they regard as their rights. Minnie Hauk and Marie Roze once feuded over the best dressing room before a performance of Mozart's *Marriage of Figaro*. At 3 p.m. Ms. Hauk arrived at the theater and placed her baggage in the best dressing room. At 4 p.m. Ms. Roze's maid arrived, removed Ms. Hauk's baggage from the dressing room and replaced it with Ms. Roze's baggage. At 5:30 p.m. Ms. Hauk's agent arrived, removed Ms. Roze's baggage from the dressing room and replaced it with Ms. Hauk's baggage—and he padlocked the dressing room when he left. At 6 p.m. Ms. Roze arrived, saw the padlocked door and called a locksmith to open the door, then removed Ms. Hauk's baggage from the dressing room and replaced it with her own. At 6:30 p.m. Ms. Hauk arrived and saw Ms. Roze in the best dressing room, and then she returned to her hotel and announced that she would not sing that evening.[233]

- Duke Ellington did not have a lot of rules for his musicians. He did not even call them back to the bandstand after a break was over. Instead, he would go to the piano and play a few dissonant notes that were easy to hear through the noise of wherever the band was performing. A few of his musicians would come to the bandstand, and they would play something soft that Duke had written. More and more of his musicians would come to the bandstand, and they would play something soft that Duke had written. (Duke was always able to come up with something soft to play based on the musicians who were on the stage. In fact, he even wrote tunes that he could play with only a few musicians.) Eventually, everybody would be on the bandstand and then they would play one of Duke's loudest tunes. Bassist Milt Hinton, who played with Cab Calloway's band, said, "The contrast was unbelievable. The guys had gotten back on their own time. They were ready and wanted to be there. So when the full band hit, the earth shook."[234]

- David Wolff, the manager of musician Cyndi Lauper, started his career as a musician, an insecure job that necessitated stints at ordinary jobs to get money to live on. Once, he needed a job as an exterminator. He knew that the person doing the hiring would not like his long hair, so he wore a short-hair wig when he interviewed for the job, which he got. However, on his first day on the job he did not wear the wig. The man who had hired him looked at his long ponytail and said, "You didn't look like that yesterday. You better be real good at this." Actually, Mr. Wolff quit after a month because he hated the straight job. By the way, Brian Wilson of the Beach Boys once ordered a wooden wall put up around his dining room and eight tons of sand put on the floor. Why? He moved his piano in the room so he could compose surfing music while feeling the sand with his toes.[235]

- Body type is important to ballerinas, and even a great ballerina can lose a role simply because her body type doesn't fit a preconceived conception. Evelyn Hart desperately wanted to dance the role of Juliet in Kenneth MacMillan's production of *Romeo and Juliet* at the American Ballet Theater; however, although she begged him to let her do the role, he would not, stating that she would be taller than Juliet's mother. Ms. Hart protested that in real life she was taller than her own mother, but this argument had no effect on Mr. MacMillan. Other ballerinas have not had the opportunity to work with accomplished male ballet dancers because of height issues. Mikhail Barynshikov often would find a talented ballerina, but be disappointed because she was too tall to be paired with him.[236]

• Modern dance pioneer Martha Graham stated that when she danced, she became the character whom she was portraying. One of the pieces she choreographed and danced was "Legend of Judith," based on the Biblical story of a woman who saved her people by murdering a tyrant. One day, she was explaining how difficult it was to dance this piece in Washington, D.C., at Constitution Hall: "There are brass rings there for electrical outlets, and you wonder if you're going to catch your toe and fall or have some sort of accident." Dance critic Walter Terry said to her, "I thought you said you never thought of anything onstage, that you became the character itself." Ms. Graham replied, "I do. I looked at those rings and said to myself, 'One more hazard for Judith to face.'"[237]

• Phil Schaap, a jazz disc jockey in New York, really knows his stuff. While he was in college, he auditioned to be a disc jockey at WKCR. Another student gave him a blindfold test, playing records for him to identify while he was blindfolded so he could not look at the album cover. Mr. Schaap quickly identified some famous pianists such as Count Basie and McCoy Tyner, so the student played someone who was not nearly as well known. Ms. Schaap immediately identified him: "That's Richard Aaron Katz, born March 13, 1924, in Baltimore, Maryland." The other student was impressed. By the way, the other student was Mr. Katz' son.[238]

• In the early 1960s, Elaine Summers performed Carolee Schneemann's *The Queen's Dog* at the Judson Church. In it, a male dancer manipulated the bodies of the female dancers, who were required to remain motionless in whatever position the male dancer put them in. Unfortunately, a member of the audience was determined that Ms. Summers not remain immobile. The audience member first threw a glass of water in her face, and then a tomato. The dirty tricks did not work—Ms. Summers remained immobile.[239]

• Ruthanna Boris—like many other young dancers—was much impressed by baby ballerina Tamara Toumanova, and so she started imitating her, even carrying her head the way Ms. Toumanova carried her head. Of course, choreographer George Balanchine knew what she was doing, and one day he told her, "Your name is Ruthanna Boris and not Tamara Toumanova, and I wish you would pick up your head because that is one habit I could not make Tamara change. It's not good for your dancing."[240]

• Thomas Beecham planned a series of concerts, but he had not yet engaged a chamber orchestra to play at them. Knowing this, Charles Draper, a world-class clarinetist, visited him to offer the services of his own group of musicians. While discussing the series of concerts, they took a walk, and during the walk, they found three horseshoes. Impressed with this evidence of good fortune, they decided to go ahead with the series of concerts, which turned out to be a great success.[241]

• Quite a few musicians started out playing in Joe Marsala's band and then left it to play in Tommy Dorsey's band, including Joe Bushkin, Carmen Mastren, Buddy Rich, and Dave Tough. When Mr. Rich left Mr. Marsala's band to play in Mr. Dorsey's band, Mr. Marsala sent this telegraph to Mr. Dorsey: "Dear Tommy, How about giving me a job in your band so I can play with mine?"[242]

• In 1940 at the Old Vic, Harley Granville-Barker unofficially directed *King Lear*, meaning he did the preparatory work but would not allow his name to be announced as director. John Gielgud played

King Lear, and he read through the entire play for Mr. Granville-Barker. After hearing the reading, Mr. Granville-Barker told Mr. Gielgud, "You got two lines right. Now we will begin to work."[243]

• At the ballet, what the audience sees is an illusion. As long as a dancer has her back to the audience, she may gasp for breath and contort her face—but when she again faces the audience, her face will be composed and her dancing will seem effortless. In the final act of *Swan Lake*, the swans have danced so hard and perspired so much that wherever a dancer sits, she leaves a wet spot.[244]

• Gioacchino Rossini could compose very quickly. He and his librettist, Tottola, worked together on the opera *Moses*. One day, Tottola told Rossini that he had written a prayer for the Hebrews in the third act—a prayer that had taken just one hour to write. Rossini said, "If you have written this in an hour, then I'll set it to music in a quarter of an hour." Rossini then did exactly that.[245]

• In the USSR, on the eve of the annual celebration of the Revolution, Albert E. Kahn went to the Bolshoi, which seemed empty. Finally, he went upstairs, where he discovered ballerina Galina Ulanova practicing. When she had finished, he asked her why she had been working on a day that everyone else was taking off. She replied, "I need the practice."[246]

• Operatic soprano Kirsten Flagstad immensely disliked cigarette smoke and complained about people who smoked cigarettes in her presence. However, she enjoyed the smell of cigars, and before singing in concerts she used to ask either her husband or Edwin McArthur, her long-time accompanist, to smoke a cigar and blow the smoke in her face.[247]

• Early in his career, Leonard Bernstein worked as an accompanist for choreographer Agnes de Mille's dance classes. However, one day Ms. de Mille's ballet master fired Mr. Bernstein because, the ballet master said, he could not keep time. Later, of course, Mr. Bernstein became the renowned conductor of the New York Philharmonic.[248]

• A belly dancer who was the evening's entertainment for a cruise picked a woman out of the crowd for a free lesson. Unfortunately, the woman she picked was professional belly dancer Najwa. After the "lesson," the passengers asked for Najwa to perform—instead of the paid dancer—for the rest of the cruise.[249]

• Ballerina Margot Fonteyn danced in Roland Petit's *Paradise Lost*, which required her to crawl through a 30-foot passage to get to a trap door. During one performance, as she crawled along the passage, she thought to herself, "This is a hell of a way to spend your 48th birthday."[250]

Appendix A: Bibliography

Alda, Frances. *Men, Women, and Tenors*. Boston, MA: Houghton Mifflin Company, 1937.

Algeranoff, H. *My Years With Pavlova*. London: William Heinemann, Ltd., 1957.

Anthony, Gordon. *A Camera at the Ballet: Pioneer Dancers of the Royal Ballet*. Newton Abbot, Devon: David & Charles, Limited, 1975.

Arnold, Sandra Martin. *Alicia Alonso: First Lady of the Ballet*. New York: Walker and Company, 1993.

Ashley, Merrill. *Dancing for Balanchine*. New York: E.P. Dutton, Inc., 1984.

Atkinson, Margaret F. and May Hillman. *Dancers of the Ballet*. New York: Alfred A. Knopf, 1955.

Augustyn, Frank, and Shelley Tanaka. *Footnotes: Dancing the World's Best-Loved Ballets*. Brookfield, CT: The Millbrook Press, 2001.

Baer, Nancy Van Norman. *Bronislava Nijinska: A Dancer's Legacy*. San Francisco, CA: Fine Arts Museums of San Francisco, 1986.

Balfour, Victoria. *Rock Wives*. New York: Beech Tree Books, 1986.

Barber, David W. *Tutus, Tights, and Tiptoes: Ballet History as It Ought to be Taught*. Toronto, Canada: Sound and Vision, 2000.

Barber, David W. *When the Fat Lady Sings: Opera History as It Ought to be Taught*. Toronto, Canada: Sound and Vision, 1990.

Beecham, Thomas. A *Mingled Chime*. New York: Da Capo Press, 1976.

Bing, Sir Rudolf. *5000 Nights at the Opera*. Garden City, NY: Doubleday and Company, Inc., 1972.

Borge, Victor, and Robert Sherman. *My Favorite Comedies in Music*. New York: Franklin Watts, 1980.

Borge, Victor, and Robert Sherman. *My Favorite Intermissions*. Garden City, NY: Doubleday and Co., Inc., 1971.

Boyden, John, collector. *Stick to the Music: Scores of Orchestral Tales*. London: Souvenir Press, 1992.

Brook, Donald. *Singers of Today*. Freeport, New York: Books for Libraries Press, 1971.

Brubach, Holly. *Ten Dancers*. Photographs by Pierre Petitjean. New York: William Morrow and Company, Inc., 1982.

Callas, Evangelia. *My Daughter Maria Callas*. New York: Fleet Publishing Corporation, 1960.

Cantor, Eddie, and David Freedman. *Ziegfeld: The Great Glorifier.* New York: Alfred H. King, Inc., 1934.

Carson, Mina, Tisa Lewis, and Susan M. Shaw. *Girls Rock! Fifty Years of Women Making Music.* Lexington, KY: University Press of Kentucky, 2004.

Caruso, Dorothy. *Enrico Caruso: His Life and Death.* New York: Simon and Schuster, Inc., 1945.

Chapin, Schuyler. *Sopranos, Mezzos, Tenors, Bassos, and Other Friends.* New York: Crown Publishers, Inc., 1995.

Chotzinoff, Samuel. *Toscanini: An Intimate Portrait.* New York: Alfred A. Knopf, 1956.

Clarke, Mary. *Antoinette Sibley.* Photographs by Leslie E. Spatt. Introduction by Sir Frederick Ashton. London: Dance Books, 1981.

Le Clercq, Tanaquil. *The Ballet Cook Book.* New York: Stein and Day, Publishers, 1966.

Crow, Bill. *Jazz Anecdotes.* New York: Oxford University Press, 1990.

Cubberley, William, and Joseph Carmen. *Round About the Ballet.* Photographs by Roy Round. Pompton Plains, NJ: Limelight Editions, 2004.

Damrosch, Walter. *My Musical Life.* New York: Charles Scribner's Sons, 1923.

Danilova, Alexandra. *Choura: The Memoirs of Alexandra Danilova.* New York: Alfred A. Knopf, 1986.

de Mille, Agnes. *Portrait Gallery.* Boston, MA: Houghton Mifflin Company, 1990.

Deffaw, Chip. *Jazz Veterans: A Portrait Gallery.* Photographs by Nancy Miller Elliott and John & Andreas Johnsen. Fort Bragg, CA: Cypress House Press, 1996.

Dolin, Anton. *Alicia Markova: Her Life and Art.* New York: Hermitage House, 1953.

Dolin, Anton. *Olga Spessivtzeva.* London: Dance Books, Ltd., 1974.

Domingo, Plácido. *My First Forty Years.* New York: Alfred A Knopf, 1983.

Donaldson, William. *Great Disasters of the Stage.* London: Arrow Books, Limited, 1984.

Douglas, Nigel. *Legendary Voices.* London: Andre Deutsch Limited, 1992.

Douglas, Nigel. *More Legendary Voices.* London: Andre Deutsch Limited, 1994.

Dowd, Olympia. *A Young Dancer's Apprenticeship.* Brookfield, CT: Twenty-First Century Books, 2003.

Editors of Dance Magazine, with text by Gloria Manor. *The Gospel According to Dance.* New York: St. Martin's Press, 1980.

Eichenbaum, Rose. *Masters of Movement: Portraits of America's Great Choreographers.* Washington, D.C.: Smithsonian Books, 2004.

Ewen, David. *Dictators of the Baton*. Chicago: Ziff-Davis Publishing Company, 1948.
Ewen, David. *Famous Conductors*. New York: Dodd, Mead & Company, 1966.
Ewen, David, complier. *Listen to the Mocking Words*. New York: Arco Publishing Co., 1945.
Farrell, Suzanne. *Holding On to the Air*. New York: Summit Books, 1990.
Finck, Henry T. *Musical Laughs*. New York: Funk & Wagnalls Company, 1924.
Finck, Henry T. *My Adventures in the Golden Age of Music*. New York and London: Funk & Wagnalls Company, 1926.
Fisher, Barbara Milberg. *In Balanchine's Company: A Dancer's Memoir*. Middletown, CT: Wesleyan University Press, 2006.
Fonteyn, Margot. *Autobiography*. New York: Alfred A. Knopf, 1976.
Fonteyn, Margot, presenter. *Pavlova: Portrait of a Dancer*. New York: Viking Penguin, Inc., 1984.
Frank, Rusty E. *Tap! The Greatest Tap Dance Stars and Their Stories, 1900-1955*. New York: William Morrow and Company, Inc., 1990.
Franko, Mark. *Excursion for Miracles: Paul Sanasardo, Donya Feuer, and Studio for Dance, 1955-1964*. Middletown, CT: Wesleyan University Press, 2005.
Franks, A.H., editor. *Pavlova: A Collection of Memoirs*. New York: Da Capo Press, Inc., 1956.
Freedman, Russell. *Martha Graham: A Dancer's Life*. New York: Clarion Books, 1998.
Freeman, Gillian, and Edward Thorpe. *Ballet Genius*. London: Equation, 1988.
Gale, Joseph. *Behind Barres: The Mystique of Masterly Teaching*. New York: Dance Horizons, 1980.
Garden, Mary, and Louis Biancolli. *Mary Garden's Story*. New York: Simon and Schuster, Inc., 1951.
Garden, Nancy. *Lesbian and Gay Stories of Struggle, Progress, and Hope, 1950 to the Present*. New York: Farrar Straus Giroux, 2007.
Garfunkle, Trudy. *On Wings of Joy: The Story of Ballet from the 16th Century to Today*. Boston, MA: Little, Brown and Company, 1994.
Gielgud, John. *Distinguished Company*. London: Heinemann, 1972.
Gielgud, John. *Stage Directions*. New York: Random House, 1963.
Gottlieb, Robert. *George Balanchine: The Ballet Maker*. New York: HarperCollins Publishers, Inc., 2004.
Gray, Hector. *An Actor Looks Back*. Hobart Tasmania: Cat and Fiddle Press, 1973.
Gregory, Cynthia. *Cynthia Gregory Dances Swan Lake*. New York: Simon and Schuster, Inc., 1990.

Greskovic, Robert. *Ballet 101*. New York: Hyperion, 1998.

Grody, Svetlana McLee, and Dorothy Daniels Lister. *Conversations With Choreographers*. Portsmouth, NH: Heinemann, 1996.

Groover, David L., and Cecil C. Conner, Jr. *Skeletons from the Opera Closet*. New York: St. Martin's Press, 1986.

Gruen, John. *People Who Dance*. Pennington, NJ: Princeton Book Company, 1988.

Hall, Marilyn, and Rabbi Jerome Cutler. *The Celebrity Kosher Cookbook*. Los Angeles: J.P. Tarcher, Inc., 1975.

Harris, Margaret Haile. *Loie Fuller: Magician of Light*. Richmond, VA: The Virginia Museum, 1979.

Hasday, Judy L. *Savion Glover: Entertainer*. New York: Chelsea House, 2006.

Haskins, Jim, and N.R. Mitgang. *Mr. Bojangles: The Story of Bill Robinson*. New York: William Morrow and Company, Inc., 1988.

Hewlett-Davies, Barry, editor and compiler. *A Night at the Opera*. New York: St. Martin's Press, 1980.

Heylbut, Rose, and Aimé Gerber. *Backstage at the Opera*. New York: Thomas Y. Crowell Company, 1937.

Hinton, Milt, David G. Berger, and Holly Maxson. *Playing the Changes: Milt Hinton's Life in Stories and Photographs*. Nashville, TN: Vanderbilt University Press, 2008.

Hogan, Anne, editor. *Balanchine Then and Now*. Lewes, UK: Sylph Editions, 2008.

Holloway, Stanley. *Wiv a Little Bit O' Luck*. As told to Dick Richards. New York: Stein and Day, Publishers, 1967.

Horne, Marilyn. *Marilyn Horne: My Life*. With Jane Scovell. New York: Atheneum, 1983.

Humphrey, Laning, compiler. *The Humor of Music and Other Oddities in the Art*. Boston, MA: Crescendo Publishing Company, 1971.

Hurok, S. *S. Hurok Presents: A Memoir of the Dance World*. New York: Hermitage House, 1953.

James, Clive. *Unreliable Memoirs*. New York: Alfred A. Knopf, 1981.

Joiner, Beth. *Gotta Dance!* New York: Vantage Press, 1985.

Jones, Mrs. George, and Tom Carter. *Nashville Wives*. New York: HarperCollins*Publishers*, 1999.

Juno, Andrea. *Angry Women in Rock: Volume One*. New York: Juno Books, 1996.

Kahn, Albert E. *Days With Ulanova*. New York: Simon and Schuster, 1962.

Karkar, Jack and Waltraud, compilers and editors. *... And They Danced On*. Wausau, WI: Aardvark Enterprises, 1989.

Kaufmann, Helen L. *Anecdotes of Music and Musicians*. New York: Grosset & Dunlap, Publishers, 1960.

Kent, Allegra. *Once a Dancer*.... New York: St. Martin's Press, 1997.

Kesting, Jürgen. *Luciano Pavarotti: The Myth of the Tenor*. Translated by Susan H. Ray. Boston, MA: Northeastern University Press, 1991.

Kistler, Darci. *Ballerina: My Story*. With Alicia Kistler. New York: Pocket Books, Inc., 1993.

Klosty, James, editor and photographer. *Merce Cunningham*. New York: Saturday Review Press/E.P. Dutton and Co., Inc, 1975.

Lawton, Mary. *Schumann-Heink: The Last of the Titans*. New York: The Macmillan Company, 1928.

Legat, Nicolas. *Ballet Russe: Memoirs of Nicolas Legat*. Translated by Sir Paul Dukes. London: Methuen & Co., Ltd., 1939.

Lehmann, Lotte. *Midway in My Song: The Autobiography of Lotte Lehmann*. Freeport, New York: Books for Libraries Press, 1970.

Lehmann, Lotte. *My Many Lives*. New York: Boosey & Hawkes Inc., 1948.

Levine, Ellen. *Anna Pavlova: Genius of the Dance*. New York: Scholastic, Inc., 1995.

Long, Rod. *Belly Laughs*. Renton, WI: Talion Publishing, 1999.

Makarova, Natalia. *A Dance Autobiography*. Edited by Gennady Smakov. New York: Alfred A Knopf, Inc., 1979.

Mapleson, Colonel J.H. *The Mapleson Memoirs: The Career of an Operatic Impresario, 1858-1888*. Edited by Harold Rosenthal. New York: Appleton-Century, 1966.

Markova, Alicia. *Markova Remembers*. Boston, MA: Little, Brown and Company, 1986.

Martins, Peter. *Far From Denmark*. With Robert Cornfield. Boston/Toronto: Little, Brown and Company, 1982.

Massine, Léonide. *My Life in Ballet*. Edited by Phyllis Hartnoll and Robert Rubens. London: Macmillan and Co., Ltd., 1968.

Matheopoulos, Helena. *The Great Tenors From Caruso to the Present*. New York: St. Martin's Press, 1999.

Matz, Mary Jane. *Opera Stars in the Sun: Intimate Glimpses of Metropolitan Personalities*. New York: Farrar, Straus, and Cudahy, 1955.

Maybarduk, Linda. *The Dancer Who Flew: A Memoir of Rudolf Nureyev*. Toronto, Ontario, Canada: Tundra Books, 1999.

McArthur, Edwin. *Flagstad: A Personal Memoir*. New York: Alfred A. Knopf, 1965.

Meek, Harold. *Horn and Conductor: Reminiscences of a Practitioner with a Few Words of Advice*. Rochester, NY: University of Rochester Press, 1997.

Melba, Nellie. *Melodies and Memories*. New York: George H. Doran Company, 1926.

Molen, Sam. *Take 2 and Hit to Right*. Philadelphia, MA: Dorrance and Company, 1959.

Montague, Sarah. *Pas de Deux: Great Partnerships in Dance*. New York: Universe Books, 1981.

Moore, Gerald. *Am I Too Loud? Memoirs of an Accompanist*. London: Hamish Hamilton, 1979.

Moore, Grace. *You're Only Human Once*. Garden City, NY: Doubleday, Doran and Co., Inc., 1944.

Neale, Wendy. *Ballet Life Behind the Scenes*. New York: Crown Publishers, Inc., 1982.

Newman, Barbara and Leslie E. Spatt. *Swan Lake*. London: Dance Books, 1983.

Nureyev, Rudolph. *Nureyev: An Autobiography with Pictures*. New York: E.P. Dutton and Co., Inc., 1963.

Patelson, Alice. *Portrait of a Dancer, Memories of Balanchine: An Autobiography*. New York: Vantage Press, 1995.

Pollack, Barbara, and Charles Humphrey Woodford. *Dance is a Moment: A Portrait of José Limón in Words and Pictures*. Pennington, NJ: Princeton Book Company, Publishers, 1993.

Portrait of Mr. B: Photographs of George Balanchine with an Essay by Lincoln Kirstein. New York: The Viking Press, 1984.

Pratt, Paula Bryant. *Martha Graham*. San Diego, CA: Lucent Books, 1995.

Robinson, Simon. *A Year With Rudolf Nureyev*. With Derek Robinson. London: Robert Hale Limited, 1997.

Rodriguez-Hunter, Suzanne. *Found Meals of the Lost Generation*. Boston, MA: Faber and Faber, 1994.

Rogers, Clara Kathleen (Clara Doria). *Memories of a Musical Career*. Norwood, Massachusetts: The Plimpton Press, 1932.

Rogers, Francis. *Some Famous Singers of the 19th Century*. New York: Arno Press, 1977.

Rogosin, Elinor. *The Dance Makers: Conversations with American Choreographers*. New York: Walker and Company, 1980.

Roseman, Janet Lynn. *Dance Masters: Interviews with Legends of Dance*. New York: Routledge, 2001.

Rubin, Stephen E. *The New Met in Profile*. New York: Macmillan Publishing Co., Inc., 1974.

Rubin, Susan Goldman. *Music was It: Young Leonard Bernstein*. Watertown, Massachusetts: Charlesbridge, 2011.

Russell, Anna. *I'm Not Making This Up, You Know: The Autobiography of the Queen of Musical Parody*. New York: The Continuum Publishing Company, 1985.

Schwarzkopf, Elisabeth. *On and Off the Record: A Memoir of Walter Legge*. New York: Charles Scribner's Sons, 1982.

Shawn, Ted. *One Thousand and One Night Stands*. With Gray Poole. New York: Da Capo Press, Inc., 1979.

Slezak, Leo. *Song of Motley*. New York: Arno Press, 1977.

Slonimsky, Nicolas. *Slonimsky's Book of Musical Anecdotes*. New York and London: Routledge, 2002.

Smith, Patrick J. *A Year at the Met*. New York: Alfred A. Knopf, 1983.

Speaker-Yuan, Margaret. *Agnes de Mille*. New York: Chelsea House Publishers, 1990.

Story, Rosalyn M. *And So I Sing: African-American Divas of Opera and Concert*. New York: Warner Books, 1990.

Sullivan, George. *Any Number Can Play*. New York: Thomas Y. Crowell, 1990.

Suntree, Susan. *Rita Moreno*. New York: Chelsea House Publishers, 1993.

Szilard, Paul. *Under My Wings: My Life as an Impresario*. New York: Limelight Editions, 2002.

Tallchief, Maria. *Maria Tallchief: America's Prima Ballerina*. With Larry Kaplan. New York: Henry Holt and Company, 1997.

Tanner, Stephen. *Opera Antics and Anecdotes*. Toronto, Canada: Sound and Vision, 1999.

Teachout, Terry. *All in the Dances: A Brief Life of George Balanchine*. New York: Harcourt, Inc., 2004.

Terry, Walter. *Frontiers of Dance: The Life of Martha Graham*. New York: Thomas Y. Crowell Company, 1975.

Terry, Walter. *Ted Shawn: Father of American Dance*. New York: The Dial Press, 1976.

Tharp, Twyla. *Push Comes to Shove*. New York: Bantam Books, 1992.

Tracy, Robert, and Sharon DeLano. *Balanchine's Ballerinas: Conversations with the Muses*. New York: Linden Press/Simon and Schuster, 1983.

Traubel, Helen. *St. Louis Woman*. New York: Duell, Sloan and Pearce, 1959.

Vickers, Hugh. *Even Greater Operatic Disasters*. New York: St. Martin's Press, 1982.

Vickers, Hugh. *Great Operatic Disasters*. New York: St. Martin's Press, Inc., 1979. Introduction by Sir Peter Ustinov.

Villella, Edward. *Prodigal Son: Dancing for Balanchine in a World of Pain and Magic.* With Larry Kaplan. New York: Simon and Schuster, 1992.

Wagner, Alan. *Prima Donnas and Other Wild Beasts.* Larchmont, NY: Argonaut Books, 1961.

Wells, Steven. *Punk: Young, Loud, and Snotty.* New York: Thunder's Mouth Press, 2004.

Wheatcroft, Andrew, compiler. *Dolin: Friends and Memories.* London and Henley: Routledge & Kegan Paul, 1982.

White, Betty. *Here We Go Again: My Life in Television.* New York: St. Martin's Press, 1995.

Ybarra, T.R. *Caruso: The Man of Naples and the Voice of God.* New York: Harcourt, Brace and Company, 1953.

Zoritch, George. *Ballet Mystique: Behind the Glamour of the Ballet Russe.* Mountain View, CA: Cynara Editions, 2000.

Appendix B: About the Author

It was a dark and stormy night. Suddenly a cry rang out, and on a hot summer night in 1954, Josephine, wife of Carl Bruce, gave birth to a boy — me. Unfortunately, this young married couple allowed Reuben Saturday, Josephine's brother, to name their first-born. Reuben, aka "The Joker," decided that Bruce was a nice name, so he decided to name me Bruce Bruce. I have gone by my middle name — David — ever since.

Being named Bruce David Bruce hasn't been all bad. Bank tellers remember me very quickly, so I don't often have to show an ID. It can be fun in charades, also. When I was a counselor as a teenager at Camp Echoing Hills in Warsaw, Ohio, a fellow counselor gave the signs for "sounds like" and "two words," then she pointed to a bruise on her leg twice. Bruise Bruise? Oh yeah, Bruce Bruce is the answer!

Uncle Reuben, by the way, gave me a haircut when I was in kindergarten. He cut my hair short and shaved a small bald spot on the back of my head. My mother wouldn't let me go to school until the bald spot grew out again.

Of all my brothers and sisters (six in all), I am the only transplant to Athens, Ohio. I was born in Newark, Ohio, and have lived all around Southeastern Ohio. However, I moved to Athens to go to Ohio University and have never left.

At Ohio U, I never could make up my mind whether to major in English or Philosophy, so I got a bachelor's degree with a double major in both areas, then I added a Master of Arts degree in English and a Master of Arts degree in Philosophy. Yes, I have my MAMA degree.

Currently, and for a long time to come (I eat fruits and veggies), I am spending my retirement writing books such as *Nadia Comaneci: Perfect 10*, *The Funniest People in Comedy*, *Homer's* Iliad: *A Retelling in Prose*, and *William Shakespeare's* Hamlet: *A Retelling in Prose*.

By the way, my sister Brenda Kennedy writes romances such as *A New Beginning* and *Shattered Dreams*.

Appendix C: Some Books by David Bruce

Anecdote Collections
250 Anecdotes About Opera
250 Anecdotes About Religion
250 Anecdotes About Religion: Volume 2
250 Music Anecdotes
Be a Work of Art: 250 Anecdotes and Stories
Boredom is Anti-Life: 250 Anecdotes and Stories
The Coolest People in Art: 250 Anecdotes
The Coolest People in the Arts: 250 Anecdotes
The Coolest People in Books: 250 Anecdotes
The Coolest People in Comedy: 250 Anecdotes
The Coolest People in the Performing Arts: 250 Anecdotes
Create, Then Take a Break: 250 Anecdotes
Don't Fear the Reaper: 250 Anecdotes
The Funniest People in Art: 250 Anecdotes
The Funniest People in Books: 250 Anecdotes
The Funniest People in Books, Volume 2: 250 Anecdotes
The Funniest People in Books, Volume 3: 250 Anecdotes
The Funniest People in Comedy: 250 Anecdotes
The Funniest People in Dance: 250 Anecdotes
The Funniest People in Families: 250 Anecdotes
The Funniest People in Families, Volume 2: 250 Anecdotes
The Funniest People in Families, Volume 3: 250 Anecdotes
The Funniest People in Families, Volume 4: 250 Anecdotes
The Funniest People in Families, Volume 5: 250 Anecdotes
The Funniest People in Families, Volume 6: 250 Anecdotes
The Funniest People in Movies: 250 Anecdotes
The Funniest People in Music: 250 Anecdotes
The Funniest People in Music, Volume 2: 250 Anecdotes
The Funniest People in Music, Volume 3: 250 Anecdotes
The Funniest People in Neighborhoods: 250 Anecdotes
The Funniest People in Relationships: 250 Anecdotes
The Funniest People in Sports: 250 Anecdotes
The Funniest People in Sports, Volume 2: 250 Anecdotes

The Funniest People in Television and Radio: 250 Anecdotes
The Funniest People in Theater: 250 Anecdotes
The Funniest People Who Live Life: 250 Anecdotes
The Funniest People Who Live Life, Volume 2: 250 Anecdotes
The Kindest People Who Do Good Deeds, Volume 1: 250 Anecdotes
The Kindest People Who Do Good Deeds, Volume 2: 250 Anecdotes
Life is Good: 250 Anecdotes and Stories
Maximum Cool: 250 Anecdotes
The Most Interesting People in Movies: 250 Anecdotes
The Most Interesting People in Politics and History: 250 Anecdotes
The Most Interesting People in Politics and History, Volume 2: 250 Anecdotes
The Most Interesting People in Politics and History, Volume 3: 250 Anecdotes
The Most Interesting People in Religion: 250 Anecdotes
The Most Interesting People in Sports: 250 Anecdotes
The Most Interesting People Who Live Life: 250 Anecdotes
The Most Interesting People Who Live Life, Volume 2: 250 Anecdotes
Reality is Fabulous: 250 Anecdotes and Stories
Resist Psychic Death: 250 Anecdotes
Seize the Day: 250 Anecdotes and Stories

---

[1] Source: Lotte Lehmann, *Midway in My Song*, p. 123.

[2] Source: Robert Gottlieb, *George Balanchine: The Ballet Maker*, p. 194.

[3] Source: Mary Jane Matz, *Opera Stars in the Sun: Intimate Glimpses of Metropolitan Personalities*, p. 203.

[4] Source: Tanaquil Le Clercq, *The Ballet Cook Book*, pp. 151, 153-154.

[5] Source: Donald Brook, *Singers of Today*, p. 115.

[6] Source: Andrew Wheatcroft, compiler, *Dolin: Friends and Memories*, pages are unnumbered. Also: Judith Mackrell, "Still dancing at 94." *The Guardian*. 9 March 2009<http://www.guardian.co.uk/stage/2009/mar/09/frederic-franklin>.

[7] Source: Anton Dolin, *Olga Spessivtzeva*, p. 27.

[8] Source: Rusty E. Frank, *Tap!*, p. 117.

[9] Source: Patrick J. Smith, *A Year at the Met*, p. 117.

[10] Source: Mark Franko, *Excursion for Miracles*, pp. 83-84.

[11] Source: Trudy Garfunkle, *On Wings of Joy*, p. 37, 60.

[12] Source: Linda Maybarduk, *The Dancer Who Flew*, p. 104.

[13] Source: A.H. Franks, editor, *Pavlova: A Collection of Memoirs*, p. 126.

[14] Source: Terry Teachout, *All in the Dances: A Brief Life of George Balanchine*, p. 122.
[15] Source: Nigel Douglas, *Legendary Voices*, pp. 216-217.
[16] Source: George Zoritch, *Ballet Mystique: Behind the Glamour of the Ballet Russe*, p. 219.
[17] Source: Rudolph Nureyev, *Nureyev: An Autobiography with Pictures*, pp. 134-135.
[18] Source: Twyla Tharp, *Push Comes to Shove*, p. 102.
[19] Source: Amy Nathan, *Meet the Dancers: From Ballet, Broadway, and Beyond*, pp. 175-176, 180.
[20] Source: Mark Franko, *Excursion for Miracles*, pp. 56, 81.
[21] Source: Joan Acocella, "Wild Thing: Rudolf Nureyev, onstage and off." *The New Yorker*. 8 October 2007 <http://www.newyorker.com/arts/critics/books/2007/10/08/071008crbo_books_acocella?currentPage=all>.
[22] Source: Beth Joiner, *Gotta Dance!*, pp. viii, 8.
[23] Source: T.R. Ybarra, *Caruso: The Man of Naples and the Voice of God*, pp. 245-246.
[24] Source: Plácido Domingo, *My First Forty Years*, p. 81.
[25] Source: Olympia Dowd, *A Young Dancer's Apprenticeship*, p. 13.
[26] Source: Barbara Milberg Fisher, *In Balanchine's Company: A Dancer's Memoir*, pp. 56-57.
[27] Source: Léonide Massine, *My Life in Ballet*, p. 70.
[28] Source: Peter Martins, *Far From Denmark*, p. 194.
[29] Source: Allegra Kent, *Once a Dancer...*, p. 141.
[30] Source: Rose Eichenbaum, *Masters of Movement: Portraits of America's Great Choreographers*, p. 210.
[31] Source: Marilyn Horne, *Marilyn Horne: My Life*, p. 144.
[32] Source: John Gielgud, *Distinguished Company*, pp. 69-70.
[33] Source: T.R. Ybarra, *Caruso: The Man of Naples and the Voice of God*, pp. 168-169.
[34] Source: Anton Dolin, *Alicia Markova: Her Life and Art*, pp. 9-10.
[35] Source: Suzanne Rodriguez-Hunter, *Found Meals of the Lost Generation*, p. 173. Also: Nellie Melba, *Melodies and Memories*, pp. 187-198.
[36] Source: David L. Groover and Cecil C. Conner, Jr., *Skeletons from the Opera Closet*, p. 142.
[37] Source: Marilyn Horne, *Marilyn Horne: My Life*, p. 87, 101.
[38] Source: David Ewen, *Dictators of the Baton*, pp. 182-183, 223-224.
[39] Source: Harold Meek, *Horn and Conductor*, p. 25.

[40] Source: John Boyden, collector, *Stick to the Music: Scores of Orchestral Tales*, pp. 67-69.
[41] Source: Barry Hewlett-Davies, *A Night at the Opera*, pp. 33, 65, 75.
[42] Source: Victor Borge and Robert Sherman, *My Favorite Intermissions*, p. 49.
[43] Source: Samuel Chotzinoff, *Toscanini: An Intimate Portrait*, pp. 37-38, 56-57.
[44] Source: David Ewen, *Famous Conductors*, pp. 102, 117-118.
[45] Source: Victor Borge and Robert Sherman, *My Favorite Comedies in Music*, p. 51.
[46] Source: John Boyden, collector, *Stick to the Music: Scores of Orchestral Tales*, pp. 8, 47-48.
[47] Source: Judith Mackrell, 'It's like wearing a big plate.' *The Guardian*. 8 January 2009 <http://www.guardian.co.uk/stage/2009/jan/08/tutu-dance-stage>.
[48] Source: Paula Bryant Pratt, *Martha Graham*, pp. 35-36.
[49] Source: Ellen Levine, *Anna Pavlova: Genius of the Dance*, p. 87.
[50] Source: Sandra Martin Arnold, *Alicia Alonso: First Lady of the Ballet*, p. 56.
[51] Source: Henry T. Finck, *Musical Laughs*, p. 14, 88, 243.
[52] Source: Leo Slezak, *Song of Motley*, p. 50.
[53] Source: Henry T. Finck, *My Adventures in the Golden Age of Music*, p. 269.
[54] Source: Rose Eichenbaum, *Masters of Movement: Portraits of America's Great Choreographers*, p. 175.
[55] Source: Maria Tallchief, *Maria Tallchief: America's Prima Ballerina*, pp. 179-180.
[56] Source: Laning Humphrey, compiler, *The Humor of Music and Other Oddities in the Art*, pp. 7, 69.
[57] Source: Grace Moore, *You're Only Human Once*, pp. 122-123.
[58] Source: Anne Hogan, editor, *Balanchine Then and Now*, p. 119.
[59] Source: Henry T. Finck, *My Adventures in the Golden Age of Music*, p. 316.
[60] Source: John Gielgud, *Distinguished Company*, p. 17.
[61] Source: Lotte Lehmann, *My Many Lives*, pp. 100, 113.
[62] Source: Helen L. Kaufmann, *Anecdotes of Music and Musicians*, pp. 201-203.
[63] Source: Jürgen Kesting, *Luciano Pavarotti: The Myth of the Tenor*, p. 60.
[64] Source: Judith Mackrell, "'I didn't want any wobbling': how to dance naked." *Guardian*. 30 May 2011 <http://www.guardian.co.uk/stage/2011/may/30/dancing-naked-peu-tendresse-bordel>.
[65] Source: Russell Freedman, *Martha Graham: A Dancer's Life*, pp. 53, 135, 140-141.
[66] Source: Samuel Chotzinoff, *Toscanini: An Intimate Portrait*, pp. 13, 19.

[67] Source: Sarah Churchwell, "Nureyev's animal passions." *The Times*. 20 February 2008 <http://entertainment.timesonline.co.uk/tol/arts_and_entertainment/the_tls/article3403291.ece>.
[68] Source: Paula Bryant Pratt, *Martha Graham*, pp. 55-56.
[69] Source: Mary Garden and Louis Biancolli, *Mary Garden's Story*, pp. 183-184.
[70] Source: Hector Gray, *An Actor Looks Back*, p. 24.
[71] Source: Jürgen Kesting, *Luciano Pavarotti: The Myth of the Tenor*, p. 61.
[72] Source: William Donaldson, *Great Disasters of the Stage*, p. 88.
[73] Source: Paul Szilard, *Under My Wings*, p. 32.
[74] Source: H. Algeranoff, *My Years With Pavlova*, p. 165. Also: Holly Brubach, *Ten Dancers*, p. 133.
[75] Source: Anne Hogan, editor, *Balanchine Then and Now*, pp. 79, 83, 97.
[76] Source: Merrill Ashley, *Dancing for Balanchine*, p. 74.
[77] Source: Merrill Ashley, *Dancing for Balanchine*, p. 14.
[78] Source: William Cubberley and Joseph Carmen, *Round About the Ballet*, pp. 6, 8.
[79] Source: Simon Robinson, *A Year With Rudolf Nureyev*, pp. 158-159.
[80] Source: Maria Tallchief, *Maria Tallchief: America's Prima Ballerina*, p. 326.
[81] Source: Rosalyn M. Story, *And So I Sing: African-American Divas of Opera and Concert*, p. 145.
[82] Source: Stephen E. Rubin, *The New Met in Profile*, p. 8.
[83] Source: Alan Wagner, *Prima Donnas and Other Wild Beasts*, pp. 206, 234.
[84] Source: Francis Rogers, *Some Famous Singers of the 19th Century*, pp. 74-75.
[85] Source: Rose Heylbut and Aime Gerber, *Backstage at the Opera*, p. 175.
[86] Source: Mary Garden and Louis Biancolli, *Mary Garden's Story*, pp. 8, 153.
[87] Source: Will Harris, "A Chat with Sir Tom Jones." Bullz-eye.com. 25 June 2007 <http://www.bullz-eye.com/music/interviews/2007/tom_jones.htm>.
[88] Source: Nigel Douglas, *Legendary Voices*, p. 169.
[89] Source: Patrick J. Smith, *A Year at the Met*, p. 118.
[90] Source: Helen Traubel, *St. Louis Woman*, p. 201.
[91] Source: Simon Robinson, *A Year With Rudolf Nureyev*, p. 61.
[92] Source: David Ewen, *Listen to the Mocking Words*, p. 41.
[93] Source: Chip Deffaw, *Jazz Veterans: A Portrait Gallery*, p. 153.
[94] Source: Susan Goldman Rubin, *Music was It: Young Leonard Bernstein*, pp. 32, 133.
[95] Source: Margaret Speaker-Yuan, *Agnes de Mille*, p. 26.
[96] Source: Janet Lynn Roseman, *Dance Masters: Interviews with Legends of Dance*, p. 43.

[97] Source: George Zoritch, *Ballet Mystique: Behind the Glamour of the Ballet Russe*, p. 127.
[98] Source: Helen Traubel, *St. Louis Woman*, pp. 136-137.
[99] Source: Henry T. Finck, *Musical Laughs*, p. 169.
[100] Source: Margaret F. Atkinson and May Hillman, *Dancers of the Ballet*, pp. 110-111.
[101] Source: Agnes de Mille, *Portrait Gallery*, p. 214.
[102] Source: Margot Fonteyn, presenter, *Pavlova: Portrait of a Dancer*, p. 93.
[103] Source: Barbara Pollack and Charles Humphrey Woodford, *Dance is a Moment*, p. 84.
[104] Source: Ellen Levine, *Anna Pavlova: Genius of the Dance*, pp. 54-55.
[105] Source: Nicolas Slonimsky, *Slonimsky's Book of Musical Anecdotes*, pp. 223, 236.
[106] Source: David W. Barber, *When the Fat Lady Sings*, p. 41.
[107] Source: Margaret Haile Harris, *Loïe Fuller: Magician of Light*, p. 27.
[108] Source: Donald Brook, *Singers of Today*, p. 200.
[109] Source: George Sullivan, *Any Number Can Play*, p. 115.
[110] Source: Anton Dolin, *Olga Spessivtzeva*, pp. 29-30.
[111] Source: Milt Hinton, David G. Berger, and Holly Maxson, *Playing the Changes: Milt Hinton's Life in Stories and Photographs*, p. 32.
[112] Source: Nellie Melba, *Melodies and Memories*, pp. 177-178.
[113] Source: Nancy Garden, *Lesbian and Gay Stories of Struggle, Progress, and Hope, 1950 to the Present*, pp. 117-118.
[114] Source: Lotte Lehmann, *My Many Lives*, pp. 196-197.
[115] Source: Robert Gottlieb, *George Balanchine: The Ballet Maker*, p. 47.
[116] Source: Suzanne Farrell, *Holding On to the Air*, p. 185.
[117] Source: Edwin McArthur, *Flagstad: A Personal Memoir*, p. 24.
[118] Source: Stanley Holloway, *Wiv a Little Bit O' Luck*, p. 124.
[119] Source: H. Algeranoff, *My Years With Pavlova*, pp. 11-12, 27.
[120] Source: Lincoln Kirstein's "A Ballet Master's Belief" in *Portrait of Mr. B*, p. 29.
[121] Source: Olympia Dowd, *A Young Dancer's Apprenticeship*, pp. 38-68.
[122] Source: S. Hurok, *S. Hurok Presents*, p. 104.
[123] Source: Barbara Milberg Fisher, *In Balanchine's Company: A Dancer's Memoir*, pp. 134, 136, 191.
[124] Source: Wendy Neale, *Ballet Life Behind the Scenes*, p. 33.
[125] Source: Ted Shawn, *One Thousand and One Night Stands*, pp. 11, 22-23.
[126] Source: Alice Patelson, *Portrait of a Dancer, Memories of Balanchine*, p. 6. Also: Holly Brubach, *Ten Dancers*, p. 133.

[127] Source: Elinor Rogosin, *The Dance Makers: Conversations with American Choreographers*, p. 71. Also: Janet Lynn Roseman, *Dance Masters: Interviews with Legends of Dance*, pp. 41, 54-55.

[128] Source: David L. Groover and Cecil C. Conner, Jr., *Skeletons from the Opera Closet*, pp. 47, 127-128. Also: Hugh Vickers, *Even Greater Operatic Disasters*, p. 76. Also: Source: Hugh Vickers, *Great Operatic Disasters*, p. 54.

[129] Source: Natalia Makarova, *A Dance Autobiography*, p. 84. Also: Barry Hewlett-Davies, *A Night at the Opera*, pp. 12-13. Also: Cynthia Gregory, *Cynthia Gregory Dances Swan Lake*, p. 20.

[130] Source: Alan Wagner, *Prima Donnas and Other Wild Beasts*, pp. 101, 104-106.

[131] Source: Gerald Moore, *Am I Too Loud? Memoirs of an Accompanist*, pp. 219-220.

[132] Source: Alexandra Danilova, *Choura*, pp. 64-65.

[133] Source: William Donaldson, *Great Disasters of the Stage*, p. 13.

[134] Source: Clara Kathleen Rogers (Clara Doria), *Memories of a Musical Career*, pp. 52-53.

[135] Source: Clive James, *Unreliable Memoirs*, pp. 44-45.

[136] Source: Robert Tracy and Sharon DeLano, *Balanchine's Ballerinas: Conversations with the Muses*, pp. 72-73.

[137] Source: Walter Damrosch, *My Musical Life*, pp. 161-162.

[138] Source: Allegra Kent, *Once a Dancer...*, p. 194.

[139] Source: Jack and Waltraud Karkar, compilers and editors, *... And They Danced On*, p. 65.

[140] Source: Edward Villella, *Prodigal Son: Dancing for Balanchine in a World of Pain and Magic*, pp. 207-208.

[141] Source: Frank Augustyn and Shelley Tanaka. *Footnotes: Dancing the World's Best-Loved Ballets*, p. 79.

[142] Source: Sir Rudolf Bing, *5000 Nights at the Opera*, p. 345.

[143] Source: Tanaquil Le Clercq, *The Ballet Cook Book*, p. 192.

[144] Source: Schuyler Chapin, *Sopranos, Mezzos, Tenors, Bassos, and Other Friends*, p. 174.

[145] Source: Thomas Beecham, *A Mingled Chime*, pp. 214-215.

[146] Source: Paul Szilard, *Under My Wings*, p. 128.

[147] Source: Gillian Freeman and Edward Thorpe, *Ballet Genius*, p. 103.

[148] Source: Stephen Tanner, *Opera Antics and Anecdotes*, p. 122.

[149] Source: Margot Fonteyn, *Autobiography*, p. 79.

[150] Source: Mary Clarke, *Antoinette Sibley*, p. 7.

[151] Source: Colonel J. H. Mapleson, *The Mapleson Memoirs*, pp. 119, 308-309.

[152] Source: Elisabeth Schwarzkopf, *On and Off the Record: A Memoir of Walter Legge*, pp. 5, 16-17.
[153] Source: Walter Terry, *Frontiers of Dance: The Life of Martha Graham*, p. 66.
[154] Source: Martins, Peter. "Foreword" to *Portrait of Mr. B*, p. 10.
[155] Source: Svetlana McLee Grody and Dorothy Daniels Lister, *Conversations With Choreographers*, pp. 172-173.
[156] Source: Joan Acocella, "Wild Thing: Rudolf Nureyev, onstage and off." *The New Yorker*. 8 October 2007 <http://www.newyorker.com/arts/critics/books/2007/10/08/071008crbo_books_acocella?currentPage=all>.
[157] Source: Eddie Cantor and David Freedman, *Ziegfeld: The Great Glorifier*, p. 24.
[158] Source: Helena Matheopoulos, *The Great Tenors From Caruso to the Present*, pp. 4, 20.
[159] Source: Frances Alda, *Men, Women, and Tenors*, p. 207.
[160] Source: John Gruen, *People Who Dance*, p. 69.
[161] Source: Sandra Martin Arnold, *Alicia Alonso: First Lady of the Ballet*, pp. 67-68.
[162] Source: Stephen Tanner, *Opera Antics and Anecdotes*, pp. 159-160.
[163] Source: Judy L. Hasday, *Savion Glover: Entertainer*, pp. 40, 47.
[164] Source: Isabella McGuire Mayes, "My feet are killing me!" *The Guardian*. 26 January 2009 <http://www.guardian.co.uk/stage/2009/jan/26/ballet-dance>.
[165] Source: William Cubberley and Joseph Carmen, *Round About the Ballet*, p. 42.
[166] Source: Steven Wells, *Punk: Young, Loud, and Snotty*, p. 21.
[167] Source: Editors of *Dance Magazine*, with text by Gloria Manor, *The Gospel According to Dance*, pp. 24, 38, 88.
[168] Source: Mary Jane Matz, *Opera Stars in the Sun: Intimate Glimpses of Metropolitan Personalities*, p. 288.
[169] Source: Robert Greskovic, *Ballet 101*, p, 379.
[170] Source: Mrs. George Jones and Tom Carter, *Nashville Wives*, p. 162.
[171] Source: Gordon Anthony, *A Camera at the Ballet*, pp. 28-29.
[172] Source: Alicia Markova, *Markova Remembers*, p. 132.
[173] Source: Walter Damrosch, *My Musical Life*, pp. 360-361.
[174] Source: Rosalyn M. Story, *And So I Sing: African-American Divas of Opera and Concert*, pp. 117-118, 120-123.
[175] Source: Sir Rudolf Bing, *5000 Nights at the Opera*, pp. 132-133.
[176] Source: Laning Humphrey, compiler, *The Humor of Music and Other Oddities in the Art*, pp. 48, 50.
[177] Source: Rod Long, *Belly Laughs*, p. 95.

[178] Source: David W. Barber, *Tutus, Tights, and Tiptoes: Ballet History as It Ought to be Taught*, p. 78. Also: Margot Fonteyn, presenter, *Pavlova: Portrait of a Dancer*, p. 110.

[179] Source: Elinor Rogosin, *The Dance Makers: Conversations with American Choreographers*, p. 68, 70.

[180] Source: Nicolas Legat, *Ballet Russe*, p. 15.

[181] Source: Marilyn Hall and Rabbi Jerome Cutler, *The Celebrity Kosher Cookbook*, p. 48.

[182] Source: Lotte Lehmann, *Midway in My Song*, p. 145.

[183] Source: Russell Freedman, *Martha Graham: A Dancer's Life*, pp. 67-68, 70.

[184] Source: Edward Villella, *Prodigal Son: Dancing for Balanchine in a World of Pain and Magic*, pp. 186-187.

[185] Source: Clara Kathleen Rogers (Clara Doria), *Memories of a Musical Career*, pp. 53-54, 231.

[186] Source: Bill Crow, *Jazz Anecdotes*, p. 236.

[187] Source: Leo Slezak, *Song of Motley*, pp. 83-84, 184-185.

[188] Source: David Ewen, *Listen to the Mocking Words*, p. 58.

[189] Source: Harold Meek, *Horn and Conductor*, p. 89.

[190] Source: Hugh Vickers, *Even Greater Operatic Disasters*, p. 29.

[191] Source: Gerald Moore, *Am I Too Loud? Memoirs of an Accompanist*, pp. 222-223.

[192] Source: Nigel Douglas, *More Legendary Voices*, p. 134.

[193] Source: Rose Heylbut and Aime Gerber, *Backstage at the Opera*, pp. 63-64.

[194] Source: Nicolas Slonimsky, *Slonimsky's Book of Musical Anecdotes*, pp. 235-236.

[195] Source: Susan Suntree, *Rita Moreno*, pp. 39-40. 49.

[196] Source: Grace Moore, *You're Only Human Once*, pp. 130-131.

[197] Source: Stephen E. Rubin, *The New Met in Profile*, p. 45.

[198] Source: Margaret F. Atkinson and May Hillman, *Dancers of the Ballet*, p. 127.

[199] Source: Victor Borge and Robert Sherman, *My Favorite Comedies in Music*, pp. 88-89.

[200] Source: Plácido Domingo, *My First Forty Years*, p. 86.

[201] Source: Joseph Gale, *Behind Barres*, pp. 24-25.

[202] Source: David W. Barber, *Tutus, Tights, and Tiptoes: Ballet History as It Ought to be Taught*, p. 56.

[203] Source: Eddie Cantor and David Freedman, *Ziegfeld: The Great Glorifier*, pp. 36-39.

[204] Source: Walter Terry, *Ted Shawn: Father of American Dance*, p. 102.

[205] Source: Terry Teachout, *All in the Dances: A Brief Life of George Balanchine*, pp. 94-95.
[206] Source: Trudy Garfunkle, *On Wings of Joy*, p. 79.
[207] Source: Victor Borge and Robert Sherman, *My Favorite Intermissions*, pp. 43-44.
[208] Source: Nigel Douglas, *More Legendary Voices*, p. 305.
[209] Source: Darci Kistler, *Ballerina: My Story*, p. 51.
[210] Source: Mina Carson, Tisa Lewis, and Susan M. Shaw, *Girls Rock! Fifty Years of Women Making Music*, p. 96.
[211] Source: Andrea Juno, *Angry Women in Rock: Volume One*, pp. 72-73.
[212] Source: Anintondrea Juno, *Angry Women in Rock: Volume One*, p. 139.
[213] Source: Agnes de Mille, *Portrait Gallery*, p. 144.
[214] Source: Jim Haskins and N.R. Mitgang, *Mr. Bojangles*, p. 202.
[215] Source: Frances Alda, *Men, Women, and Tenors*, pp. 245-246.
[216] Source: David Ewen, *Listen to the Mocking Words*, p. 87.
[217] Source: Sam Molen, *Take 2 and Hit to Right*, pp. 119-120.
[218] Source: Judy L. Hasday, *Savion Glover: Entertainer*, pp. 14, 16.
[219] Source: Betty White, *Here We Go Again*, pp. 146-7.
[220] Source: Dorothy Caruso, *Enrico Caruso: His Life and Death*, pp. 3, 67-68, 143.
[221] Source: Schuyler Chapin, *Sopranos, Mezzos, Tenors, Bassos, and Other Friends*, p. 166.
[222] Source: Anna Russell, *I'm Not Making This Up, You Know*, pp. 241-242.
[223] Source: Walter Terry, *Ted Shawn: Father of American Dance*, p. 128.
[224] Source: James Klosty, editor and photographer, *Merce Cunningham*, p. 57.
[225] Source: Gillian Freeman and Edward Thorpe, *Ballet Genius*, p. 56.
[226] Source: Twyla Tharp, *Push Comes to Shove*, p. 94.
[227] Source: Amy Nathan, *Meet the Dancers: From Ballet, Broadway, and Beyond*, pp. 120, 127.
[228] Source: Mary Lawton, *Schumann-Heink: The Last of the Titans*, pp. 330-331, 354.
[229] Source: Anna Russell, *I'm Not Making This Up, You Know*, pp. 8, 32.
[230] Source: Judith Mackrell, "Take that, Adolf!" *The Guardian*. 15 February 2007 <http://www.guardian.co.uk/g2/story/0,,2013256,00.html>.
[231] Source: Evangelia Callas, *My Daughter Maria Callas*, pp. 54-55, 72-73.
[232] Source: Elisabeth Schwarzkopf, *On and Off the Record: A Memoir of Walter Legge*, pp. 91-92.
[233] Source: Colonel J. H. Mapleson, *The Mapleson Memoirs*, pp. 65-66, 122.

[234] Source: Milt Hinton, David G. Berger, and Holly Maxson, *Playing the Changes: Milt Hinton's Life in Stories and Photographs*, p. 178.
[235] Source: Victoria Balfour, *Rock Wives*, pp. 104, 264.
[236] Source: Frank Augustyn and Shelley Tanaka. *Footnotes: Dancing the World's Best-Loved Ballets*, pp. 87, 91.
[237] Source: Walter Terry, *Frontiers of Dance: The Life of Martha Graham*, p. 122.
[238] Source: Chip Deffaw, *Jazz Veterans: A Portrait Gallery*, p. 11.
[239] Source: Jack and Waltraud Karkar, compilers and editors, ... *And They Danced On*, p. 177.
[240] Source: Robert Tracy and Sharon DeLano, *Balanchine's Ballerinas: Conversations with the Muses*, p. 66.
[241] Source: Thomas Beecham, *A Mingled Chime*, p. 90.
[242] Source: Bill Crow, *Jazz Anecdotes*, pp. 289-290.
[243] Source: John Gielgud, *Stage Directions*, p. 51.
[244] Source: Barbara Newman and Leslie E. Spatt, *Swan Lake*, pp. 119, 133.
[245] Source: Helen L. Kaufmann, *Anecdotes of Music and Musicians*, pp. 81-82.
[246] Source: Albert E. Kahn, *Days With Ulanova*, p. 4.
[247] Source: Edwin McArthur, *Flagstad: A Personal Memoir*, pp. 12-13, 16.
[248] Source: Margaret Speaker-Yuan, *Agnes de Mille*, p. 59.
[249] Source: Rod Long, *Belly Laughs*, p. 89.
[250] Source: Sarah Montague, *Pas de Deux*, p. 57.